Get Into Your True Comfort Zone

HOW TO GIVE YOURSELF
PERMISSION TO BE YOU

Susan Ingall

Published in 2025 by Dean Publishing
PO Box 119
Mt. Macedon, Victoria, 3441
Australia
deanpublishing.com

Copyright © Susan Ingall
First published in 2020 by Broadcast Books

All rights reserved. No part of this publication may be reproduced, stored in a retrieval system or transmitted in any way or by any means, electronic, mechanical, photocopying, recording or otherwise, without the prior written permission of the publisher.

Cataloguing-in-Publication Data
National Library of Australia
Title: Get Into Your True Comfort Zone
Edition: 1st edn
ISBN: 978-0-64893-865-1
Category: Self-help/Personal growth

Cover and text design and typesetting by Seymour Design, seymourdesign.net
Author photograph on front cover by Zahrina Robertson,
Personal Branding Photographer

The material in this publication is of the nature of general comment only and does not represent professional advice. It is not intended to provide specific guidance for particular circumstances and should not be relied on as the basis for any decision to take action or not take action where appropriate, on any matter which it covers. Readers should obtain professional advice where appropriate before making any such decision. To the maximum extent permitted by law, the author disclaims all responsibility and liability to any person, arising directly or indirectly from any person taking or not taking action based on the information in this book.

Susan is an inspiring speaker and thought leader who specialises in Mindset and Peak Performance. Her storytelling and outstanding content appeals to anyone who wants to achieve more fulfillment and potential in their lives. She is an engaging speaker who shares powerful stories together with tangible outcomes for any team that wants to drive performance and greater results in the future. She brings this to life by sharing the success of her clients and ensures this presentation is engaging, inspiring and thought provoking.

A message you don't want to miss.

Sam Cawthorn, CEO, Speakers Institute

I've recently had the pleasure to spend time with Susan and hearing her story about comfort zone. Now, this is really interesting because I've always been told to get out of my comfort zone, get on with life and don't get stuck in your comfort zone. But Susan doesn't say that. She talks about your true comfort zone, which is at a much higher level and you know it, and you can feel it, because she told me how to do it. So now, I am going to use the wisdom that I have learnt from Susan to get *into* my true comfort zone.

Tony Harris, Serial entrepreneur

In my time as, Regional Manager with Bendigo and Adelaide Bank Ltd, I engaged Susan to work with two of my branch teams to maximise the potential of the individuals and the branches as a unit. As she maintained accountability for agreed outcomes, I evidenced an increased level of enthusiasm, motivation on an individual basis and a greater sense of team and achievement of branch goals. Great results.

Alex Hughes, Finance Broker, FSNG Pty Ltd

I found Susan's coaching to be sharp. She kept me focused on the goals I had set. Susan is personable and demonstrates high Integrity. I can recommend Susan as someone you can trust with your life's direction. Enjoy the journey!

Wayne Donnelly; Susan Ingall was his Career Coach

Since 2001, Susan Ingall has immersed herself in personal development, creating her business, Invest in You®, to empower and maximise the potential of her clients.

Starting her career as a classical ballerina, Susan then transitioned into training dancers to elite levels in this highly disciplined art. As a former medical professional and qualified professional coach, she draws on her profound understanding of the science and mechanics of peak performance to great effect in the corporate world.

Well versed in what it means to attain a healthy mindset and a healthy sense of well-being, Susan specialises in helping her clients maintain peak performance while they transition through different stages in their lives and careers.

Susan holds a Graduate Diploma in Counselling from the Australian College of Applied Psychology and is a qualified executive coach with the Institute of Executive Coaching and Leadership. She has over 4600 coaching hours as a Professional Certified Coach with the International Coaching Federation.

Her coaching engagements include Bayer Agricultural, Bendigo Bank, Royal Australian Navy, from C-Suite executives to CEOs, as well as members of the professional services, including lawyers and doctors.

Having witnessed many clients struggling in their comfort zone, Susan has developed a 5-step formula revolutionising the meaning of comfort zone to ensure your ultimate success.

Her speaking engagements include Rotary and NSW Young Law Society, and she has spoken on the topic 'The Glass Ceiling' for International Women's Day.

Susan has recently been nominated for the Telstra Women's Business Award for courage, leadership, and creativity. She lives with her family in Sydney, Australia.

CONNECT WITH SUSAN
Website   www.investinyou.com.au
LinkedIn   Susan Ingall - Executive Performance Coach Sydney | LinkedIn
    www.facebook.com/susan.ingall
Email   susan@investinyou.com.au

I would like to dedicate my book to my children, Jessica and Camilla, who have inspired me with their childlike wisdom on this journey.

To my mother, for her wise counsel.

To my husband John, who has encouraged me all the way.

And to you, as you read this book may you tap into the full expression of who you are and live according to your highest good.

Contents

INTRODUCTION xi

1 So you think you are comfortable? 1
How secure are you in your perceived comfort zone? 3
Are you satisfied? 4

2 What is your perceived comfort zone? 11
Staying in your perceived comfort zone 11
Take your time 13
Know yourself 15
Be courageous 16
Anxiety 17
Make time for you 19

3 The first steps 27
What are you not comfortable with? 30
Don't hold back 35
Struggle 37
Opportunities 39
Stretch your boundaries – No! 41

4 Your uncomfortable zone 45
Fear 48
Comforts and discomforts 49
Recognise how you feel 54

5 What do you want? 57
Struggle versus choice 57
Achieving your goals 61
Face the fears 64
Taking action overcomes fear 66
Visualisation 68
Prepare your subconscious 73

6 Procrastination 79
Do you procrastinate? 84
Overcoming procrastination 87
Keep the end game in mind 88
The *why* 92
The roles we play 92
Reframe your thinking 94
What are you focusing on now? 97
Confidence 100
Managing the little monkey on your shoulder 102

7 What do you really want? 107
Stay true to yourself 108
When you get what you think you want,
    is it what you really want? 110
Intentions 111
Get in touch with what you really want 112
Acceptance 115
Inspire others 117

8 Who are you? 119
Creating yourself 129
Flow 139
Self-transcendence 144

9 Your true comfort zone 147
Goals 155
Motivation 160
Purpose 165
Talents 167
Your true comfort zone 168

10 Standing at the edge of your future 171
A place of freedom and fulfilment 172
Your future 173

ENDNOTES 177

Introduction

The one big question that I continuously ask myself and my clients, and will ask all of you is: *Are you afraid to step out of your comfort zone or are you really afraid to step into what I call your true comfort zone?*

It's the question I asked when my world fell apart and I had to get myself up and running again. It's the question that helped me invest in myself. It's the question that kept me investing in myself until I reached the maximum potential only I knew I could reach. This is when I created my coaching business, Invest in You®.

I previously had a thriving business as an artistic director of a classical ballet school, coaching and training students to an elite level. At the peak of my success, I experienced a low point in my life. With my divorce, I lost the family home and needed to build my life again while looking after my two beautiful children on my own.

At this point I remember holding the little hands of my daughters and thinking, I have a choice: I can either fall apart or take this as an opportunity to invest in myself and create a whole new life. I was determined to build a life and business more in line with my true values. It was a turning point for me, where I chose to evolve into someone more authentic and self-assured.

I packed the car, tucked in my daughters and drove away to create a new life. The tears were streaming down my face as I looked at the road that lay ahead, not knowing really what was going to happen. One of my daughters said, 'Don't worry, Mummy, we'll find a new home.' She said it with such gusto that I collected my thoughts, took a deep breath and said, 'Yes! We will.'

As I drove down the highway, I realised that there were two threads running through my life: I loved dance and I was fascinated with human behaviour. I also realised that we can build our life on foundations we think are solid, only to find when everything crumbles around us that it was really built on shaky ground. I needed to rebuild my life on something firmer.

I was often told growing up that I was the eternal optimist, a Pollyanna you might say, and 'off with the fairies'. But being an optimist, a Pollyanna, has brought me to where I am today. Being off with the fairies meant that I had a dream and could follow through on it, using my imagination and visualisation. When I arrived at my destination with my little family, I found a unit to rent and, with very limited resources, enrolled in a Graduate Diploma of Counselling course. Re-education was the best place to start.

I absolutely loved the course. When I graduated I continued to develop personally and professionally. Working as a life coach, I was using solution-focused therapy and emotionally focused therapy to help people. I had acquired skills in team coaching, facilitation, training and consulting. Clients started to flow to me. I created a website and ventured out, doing my thing. I felt fulfilled, on a roll and in my element. Life coaching was a natural progression, like teaching and coaching my dance students, but it was at a personal level, working with people in business and within a holistic context. The two threads, the two loves that have run through my life, dance and human potential, had come together.

You're probably wondering why I am telling you this story in a book called *Get Into Your True Comfort Zone*.

I was writing a book many years ago on procrastination – or rather, overcoming procrastination – and I was passionate about helping individuals to recognise the habits and games that were preventing them from moving through life at a faster and more effective rate. But get this ... I was procrastinating. Do you think I could finish it? I tried to give myself therapy. I used coaching techniques and exercises that were all valid, but they didn't work. Something was missing. There was something else going on. I just couldn't put my finger on it. I was being judged and jokes were flying everywhere about me not being able to finish a book on procrastination. I also felt I was being dismissed – there were so many books on this topic anyway. I decided I would take a break and see what, if anything, would come up. I'm a firm believer in giving your thoughts and brain a break and letting the subconscious do its thing. So, I stopped working on the book for six months.

'The teacher arrives when the student is ready' is something I've seen played out many times. In my case I was doing a course and my tutor said to me, 'Susan, you need to get out of your comfort zone.' I'd had enough by then and instantly I retorted by saying, 'I don't need to get out of it, I need to get into it!' This voice, what I call 'the whisper', is what I finally heard. It was what I'd been waiting for. I'd been waiting for it to rise up and shout at me. That was it. That was the answer. That was the reason for writing this book. Suddenly, the missing piece presented itself and it all fell into place.

My whole life had been an ongoing attempt at getting into my true comfort zone – reclaiming that which I had given up on. As a young girl, around the age of five, I decided I had to be someone else to survive – to be a good girl, to be strong and look after others. I lost myself in that moment. It was a result of what others were telling me and I was trusting that they knew better than me. I have spent a lifetime reclaiming myself, learning how to trust myself and reigniting passion, joy and freedom – the light that lives inside my heart.

I see the same desire in others. Teaching dance students and working with my clients, first as a counsellor then as an executive performance coach, I have noticed that most of us want to return to a sense of innocence – a time when we knew what was true and right for us.

I believe most of us unconsciously have this desire. It is the desire to step into our true comfort zone. When you do this you honour your gifts, your talents, your inherent natural genius – the full expression of who you are, aligned to your higher purpose.

I will weave into this book my story and the stories

of my clients (with their permission, of course, and sometimes with their names changed), to demonstrate the choice we all have: to stay in what you know as your comfort zone, or maybe take a few steps out of it, or begin to trust yourself to step into your true comfort zone, where you will be comfortable in your own skin, at peace knowing who you are, alive with the full expression of yourself.

Your true comfort zone is your innate talent, your inherent natural born genius. It is what you know to be true and right for you. It surpasses all else. As Kahlil Gibran says in his poem 'On Children', it's 'life's longing for itself'. When you finally get into your true comfort zone you won't want to get out of it.

I am here to revolutionise the meaning of 'comfort zone'. To make it simpler. In this book I will call the old definition of comfort zone 'perceived comfort zone' and the new definition 'true comfort zone'. You may be in your perceived comfort zone and happy to stay there, or you may have been in it and then worked on getting out of it and even made some great accomplishments. But trying to get out of your comfort zone is the old way to achieve goals and ambitions. It causes you to struggle, to waste time, energy and money. For some people it takes weeks or years, and for others a lifetime. I'm going to encourage you to go that one step further.

What would it be like to take an even greater step and get into your true comfort zone?

Come with me. It can be scary. Are you brave enough? Do you have the internal fortitude? Do you have the courage – the courage of your own convictions? Are you willing to believe in yourself enough so you back yourself no matter what? Taking this first step is the scariest part.

To help you make sense of your own journey I'll use storytelling. Stories help us reflect on the path we've taken, the events that have shaped our worldview or perceptions. As you read my journey, I would encourage you to think about your own life, how you reacted or responded, and how my journey may connect with your own story and life lessons.

In the first chapter I will use my story, and those of some clients, to explore what our traditional view of comfort zone is.

In my experience, the idea of getting out of our comfort zone to achieve success doesn't really work. It can create stress and anxiety and cause us to give in to self-doubts, fears and insecurities. I propose that there must be a better way.

So, my mission is to revolutionise the meaning of

'comfort zone', to change the perception that we have around it so that we can achieve success, freedom and fulfilment in our lives.

CHAPTER 1

So you think you are comfortable?

Many people would like to become more successful, pursue their passions and live a life of freedom and fulfilment. But they are afraid they won't be able to do it, for many and varied reasons, so they stay in their perceived comfort zone.

Living in your perceived comfort zone may not necessarily be that comfortable. You might feel warm and safe, but if you start to notice flickers of unheeded desires and find yourself dreaming of something more, something different, then I urge you to think about whether you really are that comfortable.

So what does comfort mean? The word 'comfort' has the word 'fort' in it, or what I call a 'fortress'. If you look at a fort, it has clearly defined boundaries and limitations. The boundaries are fortified to keep the people inside safe and secure.

Life in our perceived comfort zone is like life in a fortress. We put limits on ourselves and we play safe. These limits are self-made and provide a sense of security in the world as we know it. We 'hold the fort' to keep things going as normal. It's where we abide by the status quo, the old and familiar so that we feel safe and secure within the parameters and boundaries we have set.

Inside your perceived comfort zone you have:
- routine
- security
- warmth
- predictability
- short-term fulfilment.

But within these walls life can be both tenuous (a fortress can come under attack, supplies can be cut off) and restrictive, enslaving and stifling (you are stuck inside the walls day in and day out). Now, I'm not saying that it's not okay to stay in your perceived comfort zone, but what I have noticed is that most of the time individuals are longing for something else. They feel safe and secure, but they want more than that.

We put limits on ourselves and we play safe.

How secure are you in your perceived comfort zone?

For a time I worked as an intern in a rehabilitation mental health hospital. Most of the clients had gone through a major life change, due to alcohol, drugs or an emotional family issue. They were left standing with very little, after having lost their home, their family and the security of a career. They were regular people whose world had fallen apart due to circumstances they couldn't control or because they had made unhealthy decisions in their lives. They needed to start again and rebuild their lives.

For the most part, they didn't have the wherewithal to manage this enormous change, nor the emotional strength and confidence to be able to keep going.

What about you? Perhaps you are in a secure job with superannuation, a car and a regular income and you have been in this job for the last ten or fifteen years. What if you were made redundant? What would that look like for you? I have found that most of us rely on our jobs to determine our identity. How would you cope losing that?

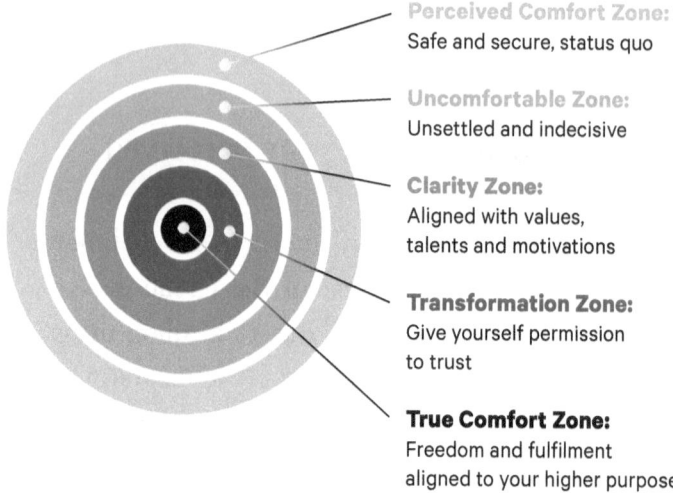

THE TRUE COMFORT ZONE MODEL

Are you satisfied?

Sitting in our perceived comfort zone, most of us can sense that there is something more to be had. We know at some level that there is something else we could be or do. Have you ever felt like that?

Perhaps you feel unsettled but can't quite put your finger on why. Flickers of ideas, questions, longings and unfulfilled dreams pass through your mind. You are somewhat lifeless or restless and you know you need to grow in some way.

All of these thoughts can be signs that you are not really satisfied in your perceived comfort zone.

Try asking yourself these questions:
- Do you dream of being in another role or place?
- Do you daydream about what could have been?
- Do you wish you could go on your dream holiday?
- Have you felt jealous when someone has or does something you desire?
- Do you ask yourself is this all there is?
- Are there things that you find you still haven't done yet that flicker in and out of your mind when you least expect it?
- Are you bursting to do or be something more?

CASE STUDY

One of my clients – who I'll call Rosie – came to me hoping that maybe, one day, she could have what she wanted.

She was living at home and had a part-time job. She was a smoker, and she had a relationship that wasn't very promising. She was comfortable in that lifestyle, it was familiar, it was all she knew, but at times she would get irritated and annoyed with herself and wished that life was different. She was in her perceived comfort zone, her comfort zone as she knew it.

When Rosie walked in I could see she was flat. She walked slowly and spoke in a monotone. She was a very attractive young lady, but came across as somewhat 'down'. When she smiled, however, she lit up the room. Instantly, I could see the potential. It was in her eyes and in that winning smile.

I coached Rosie through a goal-setting process and she realised that she wanted to get a good job and take it further – to start a career. When we explored her health goal it became apparent that she found it challenging to stop smoking. She had been smoking since she was young and her family and friends all smoked. During this session, she also realised that she had been dating men who were unavailable or not ready to commit – relationships that were not in her best interests.

During this process, it also became apparent that she wanted to travel. Rosie recognised she had limited herself and was afraid to venture beyond her family expectations, to break out of the mould. There was a part of her that needed to fly.

We came up with three goals: a career goal, a health and fitness goal, and a relationship goal. Rosie wanted to plan and start on a career path, to stop smoking and to have a fulfilling relationship.

As we progressed, Rosie started on her career path, she stopped smoking and she had the confidence to start dating guys more aligned with her values. Then I asked her what she really wanted. She said, 'To travel!' She had never been overseas and it was her real dream. Because she had worked through the coaching process, she had the knowledge about herself and the confidence to take the next step – to discover her true comfort zone.

I gave her an exercise to identify what her values were, as the way she was valuing herself was undermining her success. The aim was to get her aligned with her core values and to ensure that these values were aligned in her career, her health and in her relationship. I also gave her an exercise to identify her motivations: how she was driven. Through various questions I drilled down to find out her core motivation: freedom.

This young lady worked with me for twelve sessions. After the first few sessions she was very hopeful and excited about the prospect of lifting herself out of the mould. It was challenging. She had to address the associations that she had to smoking and replace them with healthy associations, such as going for a walk or taking a break. She included exercise for stress release and evaluated her diet and what she loved to cook. Rosie was starting to feel more confident and empowered each day, and when she entered the room for session four her energy had lifted.

One of the main challenges she had was to stick to her health goal, as smoking was such a part of her life. Everyone in her family would go out for a cigarette, offer her one and then light up together. She felt different from her family and was constantly faced with the smell, which reminded her of the cigarettes and the camaraderie that she was missing. She had to find substitutes. What to do with her hands? What to do when she was stressed? I admired her courage and perseverance, and how committed she was to overcoming this addiction. As time went on she began to see how her skin had improved, that she had a glow. Her energy levels were much higher and she felt healthier.

The other challenge that she faced was to step out of the expectations she had internalised from her family. Her parents were very supportive of her, however she needed to have the courage to make a stand for herself. Slowly and steadily we worked on her confidence, incrementally building on what she knew was true and right for her. On a scale of one to ten her confidence went from two to eight. I validated her every step of the way and reminded her of her courage and commitment to herself.

She started dating in a new way, making sure that she began with friendship and that she was respected. She took her time, and during this process realised what value she brought to a relationship and what she expected in return.

I coached her through an exercise where she created the ideal man. Through this exercise she realised that for her to have this ideal man she had to be an ideal woman. She then identified what being an ideal woman really meant and began to work on that. We had a lot of fun with this and I saw her blossom into a stronger, more confident, more self-assured, fun-loving, attractive, kind and caring woman. This process gave her every chance to realise how valuable and worthwhile she was.

More often than not, after the coaching series clients will give me a call to let me know how they have progressed. I'm delighted to say that six months later Rosie called to tell me that she had landed a job in a fantastic company and had met a lovely man. She was healthy and no longer smoking and she was the happiest she had been for a long time. This for her was her true comfort zone. It gave her the freedom and fulfilment that she had always wanted.

You see, while sitting in our perceived comfort zone we can become aware that thoughts of something better are sitting there, and they come up at times when chances are we are not really aligned to our true self, our true genius. We are deserving of something more in our life. Please take time to listen to the whisper, become conscious of it and then quietly and confidently act on it.

Ask yourself: How comfortable are you really? What is it that you truly desire?

CHAPTER 2

What is your perceived comfort zone?

You've probably heard the phrase 'Stepping out of your comfort zone'. It has become almost a cliché. But is it right for you?

Staying in your perceived comfort zone

The idea of getting out of your perceived comfort zone can sound reasonable, but it may not be what you want. It may be that you have so much going on that this would add to your stress levels and increase your anxiety to a point where it becomes unhealthy or dangerous for you.

Staying in your perceived comfort zone can mean taking the path of least resistance – not making goals or trying anything new, never travelling or meeting new people. Some people – I'm saying this without any judgement here – are happy to live like that. They feel secure and stable. They know what will happen and they don't have to feel in any way uncomfortable. Life is predictable and safe for them and they experience a level of certainty with that.

If you truly enjoy security and stability, then that is fine for you. But I'm questioning those of you who know it's not for you. I'm not talking about taking unnecessary risks. What I'm suggesting here is that you quietly consider if you are realising your full potential.

The whole idea of a comfort zone makes sense in evolutionary terms as we are wired to survive. When we feel uncomfortable it sends an alarm to our brain warning us that something might be a danger to us or could create a stress that may harm us.

In ancient times that alarm would advise us to flee, freeze or fight because there was a physical risk to us. These days that same alarm often warns us of risks that aren't dangerous physically, but which have the capacity to hold us back from reaching our full potential.

There is no judgement about our comfort zone here. It is just interesting to note how our comfort zone is serving us. Life inside our perceived comfort zone feels safe and a little like clockwork. We protect ourselves from unnecessary stress. Life outside our perceived comfort zone can be more unsettling and fearful, or challenging and exciting.

When we understand how our perceived comfort zone serves us, we can begin to appreciate who we are, what we have created, how we present to the world and why we have arrived at this point. We can also identify what our non-negotiables are. Having a financial plan to cover your needs for survival and retirement, for example, may be a definite requirement. Having health checks to maintain a good quality of life may also be a definite. Knowing your limitations physically may be a non-negotiable, depending on your circumstances. It's about understanding your level of risk adversity and respecting and working within it. We have built our perceived comfort zone based on life as we know it to date, and it has served its purpose to date.

Take your time

If you are thinking about stepping out of your perceived comfort zone it must be a carefully considered decision.

When you step out of your perceived comfort zone you might experience:
- fear
- self-doubt

- insecurities
- lack of confidence.

When I hear people say 'Leave your job and follow your passion' it concerns me as it is, in a sense, throwing caution to the wind. You must take time to think this through and balance the need you have for the routine and security of your perceived comfort zone with your need to find your true comfort zone – to be fulfilled, to be your true self. It may be that you have made good decisions and don't need to do anything more.

Everyone is entitled to time. You are not failing if you choose to take your time and consider all options, so don't feel you have to get out of your perceived comfort zone just because it's been suggested. Don't abide by someone else's time frame. It must feel right, true and real for you. You must know that this is the best thing for you to do.

Only you know what is best for you. When you know what is true, right and real for you, then you can develop the plan and be comfortable as you grow into your true comfort zone.

Some people are happy to take risks and do things in a big way, while others prefer to progress slowly and consistently. Do it at your own pace, in your own time.

Only you know what is best for you.

Know yourself

Your perceived comfort zone is not static. It is constantly changing and adjusting to both your internal and external environment. Noticing and learning how you operate is what is necessary. Practising mindfulness, going for walks or having some time out, all serve to clear your head and allow you some time to think and reflect. There is so much noise in the world that taking time out allows you to hear and listen to the whisper.

The key to reaching your true comfort zone, I believe, lays in identifying what your perceived comfort zone actually is and what your potential actually is. Then marrying the two together to create the fullness of you is where you come into your own. It's about being conscious of who you are destined to be while incorporating what brought you to where you are now. Both aspects are equally important.

Getting swept along with the romantic notion that you will be an overnight success in life or business is a mistake. It doesn't usually happen that way. It takes work, conscious thinking, planning and a length of time to build and maintain a successful life. The important thing is that you feel safe and trust the process while you are developing.

Be courageous
When I was working on my analogy of a fortress, I discovered that next to the word 'fort' in the dictionary is the word 'forté'.

This excited me, as during my dancing career I was always teaching my students to work towards their forté – their strength or natural talent. You've probably heard or used the expression 'That's not my forté', meaning 'That's not my area of expertise', 'That's not my strong point' or 'That's not my talent'.

Another word closely associated with forté is 'fortitude'. The word 'fortitude' means courage in pain or adversity. When you are moving out of your perceived comfort zone, your fortress, you need the right approach and that approach is courage.

Courage comes from the French word '*cœur*', which means 'heart'. So, when you have the right approach coming from your heart, this is having the courage of your own convictions, the courage to act on your own beliefs and stay aligned to your higher purpose. To move into your true comfort zone, you need the courage of your own heart.

Anxiety

In scientific terms, your comfort zone is any type of behaviour that keeps you at a steadily low anxiety level.[1] Imagine something you do all the time, like cooking dinner or commuting to work, or watching television. Everyday activities that you're used to doing won't make you feel anxious and uneasy, so they're part of your comfort zone.

Although anxiety isn't something we generally go looking for, a little bit can be beneficial. We often need the hint of anxiety – from a deadline, for example – to push us to get work done or improve our performance.

A classic study of mice,[2] which was conducted in 1908, showed that when a task was very easy, performance increased as anxiety levels rose. When a task was harder, however, increased anxiety only helped to a point – after a certain threshold the combination of a difficult task and high anxiety made performance drop.

The comfort zone is often described as extending into a learning zone, which eventually leads to a panic zone where anxiety is too high, as illustrated in The Panic Zone diagram. We can use this illustration to understand the results of the mouse experiment. When the task was easy, the mice were in their comfort zones – they completed the task without feeling much anxiety.

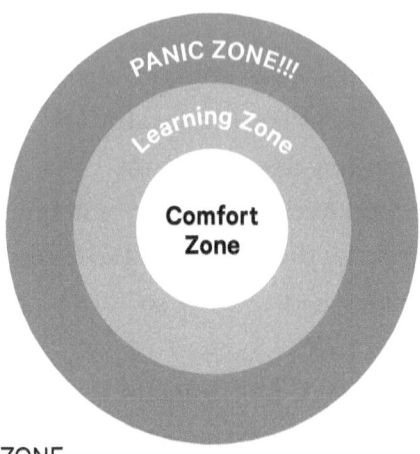

THE PANIC ZONE

As anxiety levels rose, the mice entered their learning zone and performed better. In the difficult task, however, it took more anxiety for them to hit their learning zone, and they soon hit their panic zone where performance dropped.

In this experiment, psychologists Robert M. Yerkes and John D. Dodson showed that being in a state of relative comfort produced a steady level of performance. In order to maximise performance, however, we need a state of relative anxiety – a space where our stress levels are slightly higher than normal. This space is called '*optimal anxiety*' and it's just outside our comfort zone. Too much anxiety and we're too stressed to be productive – our performance drops off sharply.

The idea of optimal anxiety isn't anything new. Anyone who's ever pushed themselves to get to the next level or to accomplish something knows that when you really challenge yourself, you can produce amazing results. This has been shown by more than a few studies. Pushing too hard, however, can result in a negative outcome and reinforce the idea that challenging yourself is a bad idea. It's our natural tendency to return to an anxiety-neutral, comfortable state. You can understand why it's so hard to move your mindset out of your perceived comfort zone.

The good news from all of this is that it is possible to step out of your perceived comfort zone. You just have to understand your anxiety levels, and have the courage and fortitude to follow what is true and right for you.

Make time for you

Taking time to really understand and know yourself fully can, for some people, be a luxury. When I speak to potential clients, I highlight the fact that most of us in our lives rarely have time to stop and take stock of where we are and where we would like to be. Twelve one-hour sessions of a coaching series over four months can make a huge impact on your future. So, why can we take time to plan a holiday but not take time to plan our life direction and purpose?

During a coaching series it's an opportunity to focus just on yourself – identify what you value and who you are being in the world, and deal with those difficult questions you may have on your mind in a safe space. It's an opportunity to re-evaluate the goals you want to achieve, and attend to the nagging little areas of your life that play on your mind that you haven't done anything about.

Techniques such as visualisation, positive affirmations and meditation are all tools that can assist you to find out what is true and right for you. When you consider taking twelve hours out of your life over three months, to concentrate just on you, it really isn't much. But the value that you will gain is enormous.

I have had clients attain promotions, find balance in their life, even write a will. I have also had clients who have had a health check that has saved them from medical problems that could have cost them enormously.

Taking twelve hours out of your life to concentrate just on you is the most precious and valuable thing you can do. Getting to know yourself and your goals, developing strategies, putting an action plan in place, having your coach hold you accountable in a pragmatic proactive way, identifying blocks you have internally or externally that might be holding you back and then celebrating your successes, especially when they are aligned to your higher purpose, is what works. And, it's so exciting.

Imagine if that will hadn't been written and you had passed away, what consequences would follow and what would that cost? Imagine if you sat in the same job for years knowing that you could have done something bigger and better and had an increased income. What would that cost, not only in your energy and your outlook on life, but in your financial life? Imagine if you had no one to check in on your health and fitness, no one to hold you accountable – what would it cost to your self-esteem and confidence?

It's not always about financial gain. Financial gain appears obvious and we can measure that. Yes, I can work with people with financial goals, however the cost of not following through on career, fitness and relationships can also be a major cost. When I talk about the value of coaching it's not just about the money you make, it's also about the things that you may miss out on because you simply haven't taken time out to address what you need to address in your life. I've also found that the freedom of choice is what most of my clients hunger for.

Taking twelve hours out of your life to concentrate just on you is the most precious and valuable thing you can do.

CASE STUDY

One of my clients came to me wanting to move to the next level in his business. He was a property developer and for the sake of confidentiality I will call him Norman.

Norman was very successful, having developed two commercial properties and businesses but found that he was stuck trying to go to the next level in his business, which was to secure another development.

When Norman called me, he acknowledged that he had been waiting for some time to finally have the courage to pick up the phone and have the initial chat with me about some coaching. He sounded full of excitement and anticipation, but with a sense of nervousness in his voice. He decided to bite the bullet and I invited him to partner with me in a coaching series.

Norman arrived looking very professional and excited at the prospect of us working together to achieve his goals. He was the father of two, recently divorced and was in the process of transitioning to a new stage in his life. As with any major change, there were questions he wanted answered, and a desire to understand more about how he had arrived at this place in his life.

When you go through a major change such as divorce, loss of a loved one or moving, it offers you the opportunity to reassess your values, your direction, your purpose and how you would like to progress in the next phase of your life. This stage can be a debilitating time. Having a lack of clarity, confidence and self-esteem can often hold you back from making the good and healthy decisions that you need to make in order to move forward successfully. Another way to look at this phase is to see it as an opportunity. Now I don't mean to sound trite when I say this; managing the grief and the loss is as valid as taking the steps to be proactive and positive.

At some level it may be that you are ready for change, a new phase. When we approach it from this angle it offers us the opportunity to really create something new and better in that next stage.

Norman had the courage to come and assess all aspects of his life so that he could move forward in a holistic fashion. In his case it was very much about providing for and protecting his children and taking care of his mother. Family mattered to Norman, as did growing and developing his business. He had already acquired new developments for his portfolio and had positioned himself as one of the best property developers in the market.

When it came to achieving his business goal he was challenged, because while he was extremely successful in his own right, he felt that he couldn't surpass his family in terms of success. He was afraid of being too successful.

Norman told me that he was struggling to land the next deal. He didn't feel confident and was procrastinating on getting it done. Sometimes we can set things up to make it look like we're doing things when, in fact, we know that there is something standing in the way. Norman had the courage and humility to admit what wasn't working for him.

Together we looked at what was happening in his life. We developed some strategies to manage his health and fitness effectively, manage his relationships, both family and personal, and then looked at developing more effective processes to enable him to be more hands-off in his business. Being more hands-off would allow him more time to focus on developing the business rather than being caught up in the day-to-day running of it. We set up systems and structures and reviewed the effectiveness of his teams.

Having reached this point, Norman found that he was comfortable – he was in his perceived comfort zone. But something was still niggling at him. You see, he wanted to expand further in his property portfolio but felt stuck in his thinking. It just wasn't happening and hadn't been for a while.

'Take yourself back to the time when you landed your last deal,' I suggested. 'What was that like for you?'

I asked him further questions, identified how he was driven and had him tell me what it was like for him when he landed the deals.

It was as if a whole other person appeared in front of me. He sat forward. His eyes were sparkling, his voice was enthusiastic and passionate, and his hands moved expressively, as he described what he loved about sourcing and negotiating, and the excitement of seeing everything come to fruition.

I asked more questions: 'What did you feel?', 'Who was with you at the time?', 'What did you see?', 'What was it that you did?', 'What impact did that have on you, your family, your business?', 'Tell me more. Tell me everything about that experience.'

I then explained that this was him at his best – in the flow, in the zone, fulfilled, wired with excitement; everything was working for him and most of all, it was easy. He was using his talents to the best of his ability and, more importantly, because of this he was succeeding.

As he spoke to me with such passion and energy, it was as if he had woken up. It dawned on him that this was who he was and that it was easy. He was in his true comfort zone; he knew deep down that this was right for him. All he had to do was give himself permission to be himself and to trust that in doing so, he would succeed. He had got it! He literally breathed a sigh of relief; it was such a weight off his shoulders. He had given himself permission to do and be the person he was meant to be and his energy flowed again. All the burden of limiting himself, all the energy he used to hold himself in an unnatural state, fell away.

As Norman rose to leave, he stood six centimetres taller and had a grin from ear to ear. He turned and shook my hand and, with a spring in his step, exited the office, focused and excited at the prospect of being himself.

And guess what? Norman landed that next deal not long after. He transformed the belief system that had been holding him back and reconnected to what I call his true comfort zone.

He went away a happy client.

CHAPTER 3

The first steps

In my experience, doubt serves an important purpose: it alerts us to possible danger or to aspects of our lives that might not serve us well. Perhaps we aren't entirely sure about something, or we don't necessarily believe something, and this causes us to hold back until we are certain. That might save us from walking into a situation that could work against us.

Self-doubt, on the other hand, can stop us from doing something that might help us to move forward. In my life, I have missed opportunities because I doubted whether I was good enough to take them on. I asked the questions: Am I good enough? 'What would others think? How will I be judged? The list goes on.

Now when I have feelings of self-doubt, I tap into my compassionate self. It's then that I am able to treat myself with care and love. This causes the negative chatter to subside and allows me to accept where I am in that moment.

A question I constantly ask myself is, 'What would love do?' It simplifies and clarifies an issue by getting to the core of what really matters. My answer would be to accept where I am in my confidence level, to support and encourage myself to take the first step towards something good, and to treat it as a learning process.

We have a choice to operate from a place of self-criticism or a place of self-love. Which way would you prefer to handle your doubts?

When I was eighteen years old, I wanted to buy a car and my father said he would help me choose it.

Now, what I had in my mind was a hot pink Volkswagen Beetle – a convertible so my hair could fly in the breeze. I'd be able to hoon down the freeway, get airborne and look really cool. Because it was pink, it was girly, and I imagined my friends in the back singing and feeling excited. It felt like it was me, really me!

One day my father came home looking very excited because he said he had found the perfect car. When he took me to see it, I walked into the car yard and couldn't see any hot pink Volkswagens anywhere. He said the car he had found was safe, secure, had good tyres, good mileage, was economical to run and if I had an accident it had a strong body around it.

Oh, cool! I thought, but then I saw it. The car Dad had found was a Torana – safe, secure, old, boring. And the colour – iridescent purple. Of all the colours you could choose in a rainbow, it was this bright glowing purple. I cringed inside. No! No! This isn't the type of car I want, I screamed in my mind. This isn't cool.

But it was safe, it was secure, and it had good tyres. So I drove home in the purple Torana. And because I am vertically challenged, I needed a booster seat as the dashboard was so high.

What I want to explain is that it's not so much about the car as about the fact that the car was safe. I was able to drive that car without feeling anxious. It was a safe. It was my fortress. It was in my perceived comfort zone.

I bought the car that was the safer option. If I had found the car that I really wanted I could have saved up some extra money, made sure that it was safe, and then bought that, but I didn't.

I hadn't worked out what I really needed in order to fully express myself at that stage. All I had was a vague feeling that it was a sense of freedom and creativity, and the fun of driving along with the wind in my hair singing with my girlfriends. I felt alive when I thought about it.

When I went for the safe option, I now realise that I clipped my own wings.

How many times do we do this in our lives? How many times do we know what is true and right for us, but we opt for the safer option? Most of us do this most of the time.

So often we limit ourselves and keep ourselves secure, rather than feeling enlivened and excited and in the flow, and being in that full expression of ourselves. It might be when we don't express our natural talent, our natural genius, or what we really want to be fully expressed, and we deny ourselves that opportunity.

Take time to think about the flicker that runs through your thoughts letting you know you may not have done anything yet about your dreams – be they dreams about travel, a promotion, or maybe you secretly want my Volkswagen Beetle! Trust that feeling, the flicker, and do something about it.

What are you not comfortable with?

You get up early, exercise, come back, have a shower, get dressed, sit down to breakfast, clean your teeth and step out of the door to go to work. Travelling to work you finally get time to daydream. You dream about what it might be like if you lived closer to your work and didn't have to travel for an hour. Or perhaps you start thinking about what it would be like if you could have confidence like Bill or Laura. Then you wonder whether it might be possible to do some extra study, but you would need to ask the boss to support you and you don't feel confident doing that.

You want to go and buy a new outfit, one like Marylou's. But you realise that to wear an outfit like that and look good you would have to slim down. So you tell yourself you're not Marylou and who are you kidding anyway. You don't buy your outfit and instead you stay in your comfy clothes.

Your mind wanders to the dinner that you had with your partner. At the dinner, they were telling you something close to their heart and you wanted to reach out and hold their hand and comfort them, but something stopped you. It felt more comfortable to sit there listening, holding yourself back from living your full expression. As you reflect on this you realise that you really wanted to comfort them and wish that you were more compassionate and expressive.

In many of these cases, such as these examples, we

can find ourselves wanting to be a full expression of ourselves and even though we can think of these things as creative, fun and expressive, we pull ourselves back, almost in an instant, to our perceived comfort zone as we ride to work in the bus or the train.

If all this is going on in our one-hour trip to work, then imagine what is going on in our subconscious mind throughout the day. If you are living in your perceived comfort zone and it is meant to be comfortable, then why are you thinking and wishing to be something else? The term comfort zone is wrong, if referring to how comfortable you are.

It can't really be that comfortable, can it?

If you find you desire something else and you don't go there, and you aren't living fully, then what are you really doing in your perceived comfort zone? What is your self-talk? What is it that you are really stopping yourself from doing to live your full expression?

Sometimes we can deny ourselves so much that we become complacent. We muddle along, never quite feeling fulfilled. If you are feeling that sense of wanting to break out, feeling that sense of frustration, feeling restless or irritated with not doing and being what you want, then my sense is that you can't be that comfortable in the true sense of the word.

I'm here to revolutionise the meaning of comfort zone, to give it a new meaning where the true meaning of comfort is represented as I see it.

In the light of this, is there one thing that you are not comfortable with in your comfort zone that you're not doing or being? What are you stopping yourself from doing? How are you sabotaging yourself? If you find these questions overwhelming, then remember that the first step is to think about just one thing. If you want to make lots of changes immediately, you might find you can't make any.

Some people condition themselves to stay in their perceived comfort zone, to live with a level of mild frustration or quiet desperation, thinking that this is all there is. They may recognise what their frustration is, but think that it's too risky for them to step out so pull back to that safe place. They resign themselves to a state of inertia.

Other people recognise their frustration and try to step out of their perceived comfort zone. But they realise they will need to deal with too many fears and so they consciously choose to return to their perceived comfort zone as the risk is too great. This choice needs to be respected and honoured as it is usually for a valid reason that an individual will retreat. Perhaps it is just not the right time, or they are still in need of something.

Some people acknowledge their frustrations and weigh up the pros and cons – the cost to themselves if they don't step out of their perceived comfort zone. They take the brave step of addressing their fears and doubts. They reframe these fears and doubts, changing their thinking about them. They can then take the steps to move through the transformation and be and do what they know is true and right for them.

If you find that at times you are discounting yourself, feeling somewhat frustrated, irritable or dissatisfied in your perceived comfort zone, then chances are you are not really comfortable. Take notice of these feelings.

AN EXERCISE

Pick one small thing that you are not comfortable with.

What do you find yourself paying attention to? What do you notice you are thinking or feeling about this? Maybe you are simply feeling neutral. Take some time to be curious and observe whether you are truly comfortable and what it really means to you.

What would you like to see happen?

What is it like for you now? What does it feel like?

What is the cost of staying in your perceived comfort zone and not doing anything about it?

What is the cost of moving forward in this situation and stepping out of your perceived comfort?

The one question I would like you to really think about is: *Are you letting things control you*? It might be a lack of money, lack of experience, lack of support, or maybe problems, situations or circumstances.

Simply notice these things without judgement.

Consider your thoughts about your situation and whether they are empowering for you.

You must be mindful as you do this exercise to be truly conscious of what your perceived comfort zone is and how comfortable you really are. The universe has a way of reading your intention and noting where you place your attention.

Energy flows where attention goes.

Zero Dean

Don't hold back

I really love networking, champagne in one hand, chatting to people about their businesses and telling them a little about mine. So when I was at a networking function with an interesting group of people, I was in what I would say is my perceived comfort zone.

I was happy and enjoying myself, everything was

flowing, so I thought. Then I saw someone in the corner who I really wanted to have a chat with and I decided I must meet that person, introduce myself. As I went to take the step to speak to them it was almost like the shutters came down. It was instantaneous. Stop! It happened in a nanosecond.

I pulled myself back and I asked myself what had just happened? There I was getting to know people, exchanging ideas. But the one thing I actually wanted I went back on in a second. The thing you want the most is the thing you are most afraid of.

By the time I finished asking myself why I was holding back, I looked over again and the lady had gone. She had gone, that moment had gone, and I had missed that opportunity. I was too busy over the other side of the room filling myself with self-doubt.

We can stay in this struggle, holding ourselves back, talking to ourselves, feeding the doubts, feeding the insecurities and wrestling with all of the things we have going on. But I believe what most of us want is to be able to get into our true comfort zone. What I mean by that is to be able to trust ourselves and do what we know is true, right and real for us – where opportunities flow, where we are feeling fulfilled and satisfied, on a roll, in our true nature or genius zone.

Have you ever had that little flicker of doubt like I did? It may be that you want to reach out and speak to someone at a networking function, or perhaps you would like a promotion, to go on holiday, to paint or draw, to study something new, or maybe you'd like to meet a nice partner or buy a new car.

Do you have those moments? We can get these little flickers and then suddenly, we pull back. What happened in that moment when I pulled back is that I chose to stay in my perceived comfort zone. I was in that struggle mode, filled with doubts, fears and insecurity. These little gremlins raise their heads, chat away at you and hold you in the struggle. Sometimes, it can be for a day, a week, a year or in some cases a lifetime. At some point you have a choice to make – you can stay in your perceived comfort zone, or you can start taking steps out of it and into your true comfort zone.

Struggle

Oh boy, have I done a lot of this in my business, Invest in You®! I created my business because I saw a need to empower individuals to succeed in all areas of their lives without wasting too much time, effort and money in this state of struggle. Struggle can cause a great deal of suffering if you stay in that state for too long.

If you are suffering in this way, then seek a counsellor, a coach, and/or a meditation group to heal yourself and move through these stages effectively and with grace.

Most of my coaching clients, from students to CEOs of large organisations, have found themselves in this state. Some are in it for a day, a week, or a year and others a lifetime. My purpose in my work is to free people from this pain, by addressing their fears, anxieties and doubts, and we need to do this effectively.

My mission is to help people let go of the struggle. And if something comes up, then trust that you can handle it. You must choose to surrender to what you really want for a fulfilled life, whatever that may be for you. Give yourself permission to have it all – to have what is true and right for you.

You see, in our quiet moments we all know what is true and right for us. So be brave. Without this insight into how we can choose to surrender to our dreams, we would always have to struggle to reach our limits, to experience the vast creativity accessible to us.

Many of the great writers, dancers, poets, scientists, healers and leaders of the world led extremely troubled lives that gave them the opportunity to humble themselves, to let go and to surrender. With these valuable insights of personal success, you can let go without so much misery, pain and struggle.

When you understand this, you connect to your true self. You need only to stay true to what you really want, do your best in each moment, and events and opportunities will appear to fulfil your desires.

I was told once that I should work out what I wanted, set the plan, work steadfastly towards it and, the most important thing, be open to the idea that with time and your own commitment, it would all work out. Realise that perhaps there is nothing really holding you back. And if something comes up, then trust that you can handle it.

When you approach your goals in this way, you do not have to struggle so much. Take action and do your best. Trust in yourself and believe in what is possible.

Opportunities

As you sit in your perceived comfort zone, you may notice opportunities that present themselves to you. If you come across or notice opportunities remember to treat them with respect. You don't necessarily have to do anything at this point, simply observe and respect what is coming into your life and what is moving out of it. We have filters on and just becoming aware of them is the first step.

Some people live a conditioned-based life: they condition themselves to accept the situation they live in. It is familiar. It is what they know. Question – is this all there is? I suggest you consider living a vision-based life, that is, you follow what you know is true and right for you, what is aligned to your higher purpose. You have a chance to create your own reality in whatever capacity that is for you.

Imagine that you are at work and doing quite well and your supervisor recognises that you might want to join the team meeting. It's the first time for you and you nervously walk into the room full of anticipation and excitement at the prospect of being given the chance to prove yourself in some capacity. You gingerly take your seat at the boardroom table and you watch as each member comes in. Some welcome you, some look quizzically at you and some just take their seat.

Even this simple step can be daunting. But what I propose is that you focus on the fact that you really feel you belong in the room – you are meant to be there. The timing is right and it's okay. You have turned up; you are fifty percent of the way there. Give yourself permission to be in the meeting.

When you feel your body relax, when you just drop into the experience, trust and be fully present, then chances are you are in your true comfort zone and, in this case, feeling fully engaged.

When it is true and right for you, being in your true comfort zone supersedes any of the glances and quizzical looks. It just is.

Stretch your boundaries – No!

I don't believe you need to stretch the boundaries of your perceived comfort zone. This zone is what you have created to keep yourself safe and secure. Everything within it is familiar and predictable. This helps you survive, and survive you do.

Your perceived comfort zone is a culmination of all your life experiences, and what you now believe about yourself regarding what you can and can't do. All you have done and not done, all the decisions you have made, have brought you to this moment based on your beliefs about your life so far. It is based on your perception of your comfort zone, not on your potential and the possibilities to be found in your true comfort zone.

I am here to transform your thinking and perception about the meaning of comfort zone. You don't have to 'push the boundaries'. You don't have to take a 'leap of faith'. You don't have to scare yourself, or push yourself out of anything, especially your comfort zone, to be fulfilled and successful. There is another way.

I challenge you, to instead of trying to get out of your perceived comfort zone, merely to reframe your thinking and gently step into your true comfort zone.

As I explained earlier, your perceived comfort zone is a place where you experience low levels of stress and anxiety. It's a natural state we need to retreat to sometimes as it is familiar. Is it maximising your potential? Do we have to force ourselves out to maximise our potential? I think not.

Author Neale Donald Walsch says, 'Life begins at the end of your comfort zone.'[3] He echoes several other writers in this area. I believe life begins in our true comfort zone. That is where freedom, success and fulfilment are found. There is no separation.

Being productive is a result of being aligned with your talents and capabilities, therefore increasing the possibility of excelling. You will be able to deal with unexpected changes and challenges because you are coming from a place of trust, your higher purpose. Creativity abounds according to your natural genius, not because you have to face a fear in a forceful way, but because you tap into the innate talent that is lying dormant.

You see, the potential is already there, I just provide a

process to assist you to access your higher purpose with ease and grace. You don't have to leap, jump, stretch or push anything. It has nothing to do with being out of your comfort zone. It has everything to do with being in your true comfort zone.

Most of us look to the outside, but I'm challenging you to look inside. Uncover the layers, discover the essence of who you are and trust that!

Think of all the things you say 'no' to, even before you give them a go, and write that list. What makes your heart sing? Maybe it is to book a Japanese restaurant, throw a party, buy a new outfit, save for a car or have a family holiday. Learn to allay your fears in a gentle, accepting way. Set aside the distractions and noise. Simply focus on what you want and take steps to actualise it.

Notice what you say to yourself. Are you remembering to show yourself compassion? Are you encouraging yourself to simply try again? If you make a mistake, how caring and forgiving are you to yourself?

As you do the little things that you want and start to evolve into who you are, you will find that it gets easier. You will be able to build trust in yourself and develop your confidence.

CHAPTER 4

Your uncomfortable zone

Making your dreams a reality requires you leaving the cosy environment of your perceived comfort zone and challenging yourself on a regular basis.

When you are in your perceived comfort zone you are in your fortress protected by thick walls that are there to keep you safe. Stepping out of that perceived comfort zone means leaving the security of the fortress, stepping through the giant gates, walking across the drawbridge and away from the protection of those walls. This is your uncomfortable zone. This is where you can grow.

Staying comfortable doesn't stimulate a growth mindset or honour you as the person you were meant to be. As personal and professional development expert Professor Brian Tracy says, 'You can only grow if you are willing to feel awkward and uncomfortable when you try something new.'[4]

But when you step out of your perceived comfort zone fears may come up about stepping into the unknown. You may doubt yourself and question your abilities. You might fear failure or disapproval, or you may actually fear success. Thinking about these obstacles can start to paralyse you so that you may actually freeze and do nothing. Researcher Brené Brown tells us that 'the more afraid we are, the more impenetrable our comfort zone's buffers become'.[5] But when you are afraid of stepping out, you are simply unaware of how capable you are.

Familiarity is comfortable and enjoyable, so it's no real surprise that new things get our guard up. Psychologist Dr Raj Raghunathan explains that from an evolutionary perspective, we see familiar things as more likely to be safe and so we're more drawn to what we know.[6] The brain thinks, Hey, we've tried that before and I didn't die. So it is probably safe to do it again.

If you take bite-size steps towards doing something new, and commit to taking them daily, you will find that the fear will start to diminish. It means stepping a little further away from the walls of your fortress every day.

Trying new things takes energy, so if you are feeling tired or flat you are more likely to slip into old habits than take a new risk. So it's important to pace yourself and not try and do too much at once.

Getting comfortable with the uncomfortable is the best way forward. That means getting used to the mild anxiety of stepping away from the walls and exploring new territory. It is new and different, and you will need reassurance that you are on the right path and doing the right thing as you go along.

You may need to develop confidence and new skills to manage whatever your goal is. Enlisting people you can trust to help you learn these and to get support and encouragement is the best way to keep yourself productive and on track.

When you start to feel uncomfortable, reassure yourself of what is in place and then work on the one thing that is making you feel that way. This will help to stop you from feeling overwhelmed. Be careful not to have an all or nothing approach. Bite off small pieces and chew, chew, chew.

When you prepare yourself for the challenges then you will have a better chance of succeeding and producing extraordinary results. Before you know it, you will be building on these results and becoming more confident.

Getting comfortable with the uncomfortable is the best way forward.

Fear

F.E.A.R. is an acronym for False Evidence Appearing Real. There's usually no true threat of immediate physical danger, no threat of a loss of someone or something dear to us, actually nothing there at all. F.E.A.R. is an illusion. Something we fabricate in our minds and pretend is real.

The energy that accompanies fear is the same as the energy accompanying excitement. Every time I went to dance on stage I would be overcome with fear as I waited in the wings. The adrenaline would be pumping and at that moment I had a choice. I could retreat into the fear state or I could expand and enjoy the excitement of going on stage. When you feel fear, think about the excitement, in my case the excitement of the audience watching me dance and applauding my performance. Focus on the excitement, not the fear.

I was giving a talk on stepping into your true comfort zone and part of it was about the effects of getting out of your perceived comfort zone. I felt I was doing okay until I took one extra step and fell off the stage!! Yes, I stepped back and fell off.

I was momentarily embarrassed, but because of my ballet background I instantly sprang back up on the stage, regained my composure and kept going, as I would if I fell in dance. The audience were concerned that I may have hurt myself. I instantly blurted out, 'Well, that was certainly getting out of my comfort zone', and they laughed whole-heartedly with me.

You see, I could have thought myself a fool and been embarrassed, and focused on my feelings and concerns. But when you focus on the other, be it a cause, an audience or a client, you can do wonders.

I learnt to measure my stage movements after that. I also learnt to laugh at myself, I learnt to have compassion and I learnt that the audience was forgiving and cared for me – and had a sense of humour!

I could have retreated and thought that I'm never making a fool of myself again, but that would have meant I would have lost my confidence. I just got right back on the horse again. I was able to not take myself too seriously and to build on that experience and have fun with it.

Comforts and discomforts
Looking out of the window of the fortress you can see new possibilities but also threats.

What is it like? How do you pay attention to the stress and anxiety?

The secret is to develop curiosity. Approach what you are doing with a beginner's mind. Develop the capacity to be with yourself.

Observe yourself as if on stage. See yourself from the balcony of the theatre. Take time to practise regulating your emotions. Catch yourself as you react. You may jump to do something, anything just to get away from discomfort. I think as an adult I expect myself to either know things or to learn them quickly and when I don't, I become very impatient with myself. For me, being patient and asking for help is one of my greatest lessons when moving out of my perceived comfort zone and feeling in the discomfort state. For that is all it is, a state of discomfort. It does not define who I am.

As you move outside of your perceived comfort zone, what was once scary and unknown evolves into becoming your new norm. When you look back at what you may have struggled with in the past and how you overcame the adversity or difficulty, it is reassuring to realise that you can work your way through it and succeed. You can become less afraid of challenges or failures as they are only a part of the process.

Maintaining a fresh perspective and a proactive

positive attitude is what I believe always helps you get through. As a child is filled with wonder and curiosity about something new, we can also adopt this approach. A child naturally has a can-do attitude.

Sitting in the uncomfortable zone for a while affords you the opportunity to assess how you are going, to assess what your strengths, natural talents and vulnerabilities are. What can you put in place to enhance your talents and develop strategies to manage your vulnerabilities? If you make a mistake, what can you learn? How do you make a change for the better? This discomfort is exciting as it allows you to realise that there is more to you than you thought.

Quite often other people can see what your life lesson might be and will support you to learn from it and move through it, so that you can continue to add value to your life.

Usually when you want something worthwhile it will involve hard work, perseverance and some discomfort. But if you believe in yourself and push yourself to complete a task or project, then you reap the rewards and you can feel a sense of satisfaction and renewed confidence and fulfilment.

If you have a Big Hairy Audacious Goal (BHAG),[7] my advice is to break it down into a daily system rather than striving to achieve it all at once. Chances are you will be in a state of discomfort for a while, but you will gradually grow into it. Incorporate it as part of your daily life and slowly and steadily it will eventuate.

You will not be the same person when your goal is achieved, and you should be prepared for that. It may be that you need to be more assertive, more confident, even improve the way you dress – it takes time to make these changes.

Take the time to really get to know yourself in this uncomfortable state. It is full of gems and life's blessings.

AN EXERCISE

This exercise will help you clearly define your comforts and discomforts.

Draw a circle and draw or write inside the circle all the things you are comfortable with.

Outside the circle draw or write all the things that are worth doing but you are afraid of doing.

What barriers do you want to get past or overcome?

List your discomforts and see what is really going on. What are you afraid of?

You might want to start networking, for example, but you find social situations difficult to handle. You worry that you won't know what to say, you lack confidence or you are afraid of being ignored.

Fear of failure can hold us back, but conversely fear of success can too. If you try something and fail, treat the failure as a lesson and then build on it to succeed next time. You are simply learning how to do it better next time. Don't get too hung up on getting it right straight away.

Take baby steps and ask someone to support you. If you take a step that is too large, too challenging, then you may retreat and lose confidence.

Another way to improve your chances of success is to join a group of people who are doing what you want to do and enlist their support. Their encouragement will help you through the uncomfortable zone.

Sometimes when we are in the uncomfortable zone, we resort to dropping back to our perceived comfort zone because we don't like being uncomfortable. Have you noticed how hard it is when you haven't exercised over the last part of winter and have to don your gear and get back to the gym? For a time, you feel the discomfort, but if you keep turning up you start to notice an improvement in energy and away you go!

So, master your fear of being uncomfortable and you master yourself. Keep yourself comfortable in your uncomfortable zone and you will manage that state much better.

Recognise how you feel

A sure sign that you are avoiding discomfort is when you use food, alcohol or retail therapy to make yourself feel better. Recognise this; pause, take a breath and reassess what you really need for yourself in that moment. Maybe you are lonely and need to call a friend, are cold and need to put a jumper on, are thirsty rather than hungry. Or maybe you need a good meal and a good night's sleep.

Watch yourself as you get uncomfortable so that you can learn to handle it. Do you have negative thoughts? Complain to others? Are you looking for ways to avoid it? Where do you turn to? What happens if you stay and don't do anything? When you master being uncomfortable then you have a better chance at mastering procrastination.

Stay with a task when you feel discomfort and see how much you can accomplish. Be determined to get past it. Treat it as an exercise. At the moment I would rather be outside in the sun going for a walk with friends, but I am determined to finish this chapter today and send it to my editor. Yes, I feel the energy rising in me, but I am acknowledging it and redirecting it into my typing. I'll let you know how long I can sit.

My driver defines me as an energy fanatic. I find it very hard to sit on my butt all day and do this, but I am observing and sticking to the outcome that I want for myself so that I can do more speaking and coaching, which is my true comfort zone. This is just about observing and being aware of the games we can play with ourselves to avoid being uncomfortable.

AN EXERCISE

- Eat only healthy food for a while and notice how much better you feel.
- Wake ten minutes earlier than usual each day and see how it becomes more comfortable and what benefits you receive.
- Clear the clutter from around your home or office as it is a form of procrastination – dealing with it is not comfortable.
- Empty your inbox.
- Do things that are free or inexpensive (which can be a discomfort in itself), so you can save and get out of debt.

Accept that being uncomfortable is part of life, keep your eye on the end game and learn to delay gratification – it's a great skill.

When in doubt, check in and ask yourself, 'What is it that I really want and is this aligned to my highest good, my higher purpose?'

CHAPTER 5

What do you want?

I was once told that the antidote to being a victim in any situation is to be the creator. And it works!

As you are coming out of your uncomfortable zone you may be met with internal negative chatter going on in your head. It can be in the form of blaming others or situations, or believing that life just happens to you. You might experience the debilitating effect of fear, or feel insecure about who you are and whether you have the confidence to follow through on your goals or ideas.

Struggle versus choice
Some people will choose to stay in this struggle of fears, and doubts for days or years – and, for some, a lifetime.

And others will choose differently. They will accept that their current beliefs are holding them back and enlist help to change their perspectives so that they operate from a more positive world view. They will call on the courage needed to do so and love themselves enough to hold firm. This is when you are given the opportunity to be the creator of your life.

When you are the creator then you do have a choice. You can build your life on new ground. Ground that is more authentic, solid and reliable. Ground that is more aligned to your true comfort zone.

Getting clear on who you are, what you stand for and don't stand for, what you will accept and won't accept, is paramount to feeling confident in yourself.

When you are moving into the clarity zone it is an opportunity to take time for yourself and get clear about your values, motivations and natural talents. Using meditation and mindfulness can assist you with getting clear, as there is no distraction and it's where you hear the whisper. You will learn to live with a greater awareness, meet your needs and feel empowered.

Understanding your true identity and what your life lessons are will assist you in fulfilling your potential. Let go of the drama, the stories that don't serve you anymore. Take personal responsibility by addressing your beliefs and supporting yourself in what is most meaningful and fulfilling for you. Develop strategies more aligned to your talents and your higher purpose

As you stand on the bridge between perceived comfort zone (fort) and your true comfort zone (forté) you have the opportunity to get the clarity needed to move into your forté, your true comfort zone, where you are aligned to your higher purpose.

Take charge and create!

It is possible to take charge of your life. You have a choice. There is assistance and support available to go to the next stage in your life. All you need to do is take the first step to start to build your confidence. And stay committed to you, as anything else is not for negotiation.

The 'Wheel of Life' is a great exercise to help you see where you may not be fulfilled. It is composed of twelve segments that together describe each aspect of your life as a whole. Taking the centre of the wheel to be zero percent and the outer to be 100 percent, mark in the first wheel where you are now in each area. At the completion of this book, take a moment and mark in the second wheel where you are.

Rate your level of fulfillment in each section from zero percent to 100 percent, creating a new outer edge.

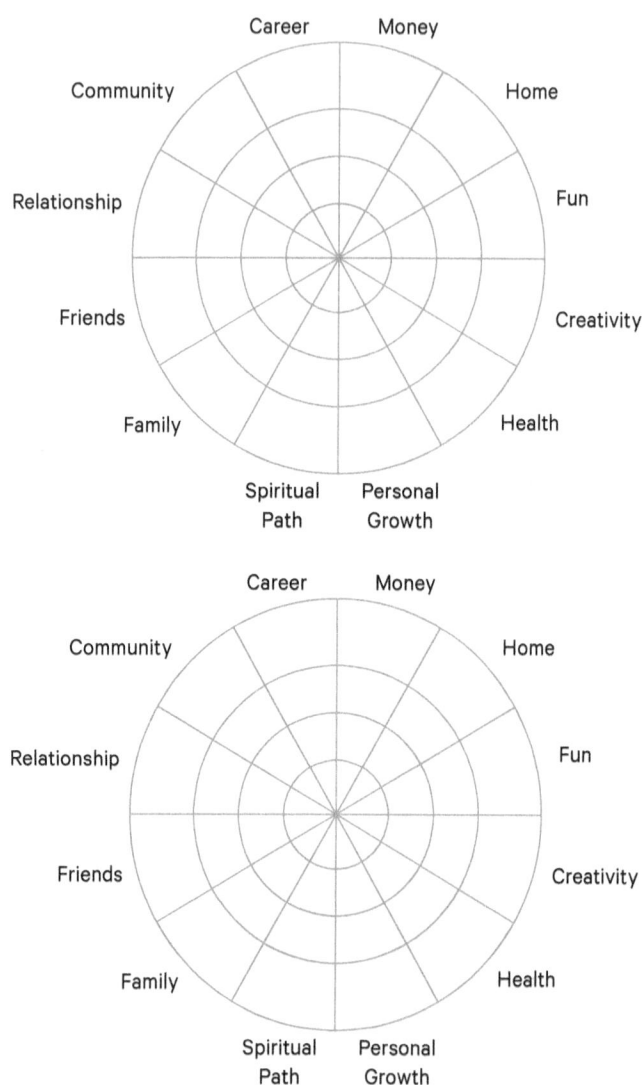

THE WHEEL OF LIFE

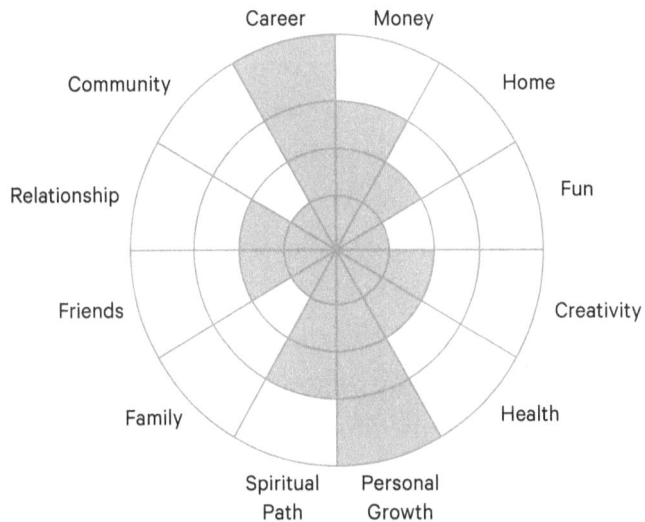

THE WHEEL OF LIFE EXAMPLE

The new outer edge demonstrates your wheel of life. The aim is to have them all at a similar level.

Once you have done this, take a look at what areas need to be increased so that you find balance and fulfillment in your life. This is an effective tool to assist you in setting relevant goals and to be really clear about what you need to focus on moving forward.

Achieving your goals

When you achieve your goals, you will not be the same person as you were before. With every stage of growth in your transformation into who you really are meant to be, you are likely to be letting go of something old. For some people that can be very scary, for others it's a relief. So take a moment to think about these questions: Are you ready for that? Who will you be? What will be going on around you? Who will be in your sphere? Who has moved away?

These are some of the things that can immobilise you when endeavouring to go for what you really want. It's worth taking some time to think about these points when considering what you want to achieve, as it may affect the outcome.

As part of my growth, in 2016 I had to choose between the job I had at the time and pursuing my career as a coach, author and speaker. I wanted to have both, especially because I enjoyed working with my colleagues. But for all my efforts to remain connected to them when I left my job it just didn't happen.

It took me some time to realise that I was moving in a different direction. My energy was changing and this meant I was attracting different people into my life. It goes without saying that I really do value my previous circle of friends and the valuable lessons they taught me. And it was just as much their movement as it was mine.

Letting go gently and with love is what is required to

allow for personal growth. And yes, it can be sad, as we would often like to keep everything the same and take everyone with us. For me to become more of who I am, I had to accept that it was time to move on.

I wanted to take the leap and be a successful fulltime coach, and with that there was a cost. The costs were risking financial security and independence and the emotional cost of letting go of the friendships and camaraderie at my workplace, which I still miss. Letting go again and writing this book while still coaching and starting on the speaking circuit has made me both nervous and excited. But I know that this is what I was meant to do.

When I say to you that when you achieve your goal you will not be the same person, I am really asking you to think about who you are becoming. More confident? More courageous? Developing increased strength of mind to follow your destiny? It's worth a thought so that you are prepared for what can happen. If it is good for you then it will be good for all concerned.

Instead of asking, 'What are my goals?', ask yourself, 'Who will I become when I achieve my goals?' If you like what you envision, then go for it.

Face your fears

When mixed with the feeling of success, a little anxiety can help you to grow. This is why outdoor adventures like abseiling, rock climbing and skydiving can be so exhilarating – they make us feel anxious, but when we complete them it gives us a huge feeling of success and increases our levels of confidence.

In 2000 I stayed on a health farm. One of the activities was to go on a flying fox and fly through the trees. In my personal development, I was a two out of ten. Trusting the equipment was one thing; looking through the trees and not seeing the end was something else entirely. I was feeling relatively okay while they strapped me in, somewhat uncomfortable but okay, until the instructor said to come to the edge.

I gingerly tiptoed over to him. Then he said, 'Are you ready?'

Whooooo! Hang on a minute. My heart was racing, my hands were sweating and with each breath I struggled to get my lungs anywhere near full of air.

It's okay. It's only fear! I told myself. Feel the fear and do it anyway – Susan Jeffers wrote a whole book about it.

'I can't do it, I can't, I can't!'

I had heard all of my team members scream with delight, but I was petrified. Why on earth was I doing this to myself? So, I started talking to myself again.

'The others could do it. Just trust. Imagine the feeling of flying. Hold on and shut your eyes and hope for the best. Feel the fear and do it anyway!'

I was so busy talking to myself that I hardly heard the instructor ask again, 'Are you ready?'

I must say, giving me the option wasn't a good idea, because I was then thinking about whether I actually was. I could have chatted to myself about it all day.

Then it was time. You know that feeling when you just have to do something. People were getting impatient with me as they were waiting for their turn. The instructor looked me in the eye and said, 'You'll be fine.' At that point, tears of fear rolled down my face. This was real fear at its worst.

Enough! I stepped forward, closed my eyes and hung on tight. I felt the push and the feeling of being airborne, strapped in and hanging on for dear life, then, hold on a minute, I was flying through the rainforest when I realised that my eyes were shut.

I didn't want to miss the view!

I opened my eyes and saw the trees flying past. I couldn't see the end. It was like going into a mass of greenery. I let out the most incredible scream. I had never screamed so loud in my life. To hear my voice come from the depths of my gut was amazing. I bellowed it out. But it was so meaningful and so real it didn't matter.

I was screaming my lungs out with my eyes wide open, and I could experience it all: the wind was blowing in my face, the air was cool and the sun was shining. It was a perfect day to fly through the trees.

I saw the people at the end all cheering me on and I was so excited as I came in to be caught by the instructor (and he was cute). Oh my God! I did it. I actually did it! I looked back to see where I had come from. I had changed so much between the top and the bottom, from shrinking with fear to being open and excited, grinning from ear to ear.

My team all welcomed me with open arms and hugged me and sang my praises. I had never experienced anything like that before. And you know what, I could have done it again. Yes, again!

Isn't it interesting all the stages of fear that I went through to achieve my goal? And I chose to put myself in that position. At some level, I knew it was right for me; I was ready to 'feel the fear and do it anyway'.

Taking action overcomes fear

The person I had to become was courageous, trusting

and willing to accept support and encouragement. I had to acknowledge my chatter, accept it and still be courageous enough to step forward. I had to be brave enough to open my eyes and take in the experience. I had to go for it. For the first time in my life I really heard my voice ring through my whole body and it was fantastic.

I tell you this because I really wanted to do the flying fox. I wanted to overcome the fears associated with it in my mind and learn from the experience, because overcoming a specific fear can help us face other anxieties. Most people have a certain medium through which they can learn to face fear in general. It may be acting on stage, it may be public speaking, it may be adrenaline sports. Whatever it is, we are here to understand our ways of operating and how we can grow.

When I coach my clients, I have the opportunity to show them how to become conscious of their fears and then build strategies to manage them, so that they continue to develop personally. One fear in particular that bears mentioning is the fear of success. Yes, success.

Fear of success is very real when we are contemplating change in our lives. It is often a fear of achieving the very thing that we most want. It is usually based on the fear of the unknown, and it can prevent you from taking action.

Getting a promotion in an organisation, for example, may bring up fears around aloneness and having to do things that some people might have trouble accepting, like needing to assert yourself more. It could be fear of being acknowledged for your potential: that you have what it takes after all. Or perhaps you may not want to be burdened by success and the special treatment that comes with it.

Working on getting your fears into perspective will help with this one. Identify what is likely to happen, and put some strategies in place around the new thoughts and beliefs that you will need to handle your success successfully. If you do this, you will have a better chance of becoming the person you are meant to be. You will be able to embrace success instead of fear it.

Visualisation

Staying focused on what you do want so that you can stay aligned to your higher purpose takes conscious effort. The mind is interesting. It often focuses on what we don't want rather than what we do want. When you are taking steps to move out of your perceived comfort zone and towards your true comfort zone, you need to focus on what you do want. You need to visualise it. When we visualise we train our brain and stretch our mind to make room for our deepest desires.

Michelangelo said about his statue of David: 'I saw the angel in the marble and I carved until I set him free.' He could visualise David, and so he was able to achieve his ambition of creating this beautiful sculpture.

When we visualise reaching a goal we become all consumed in having what we most desire. This activates the subconscious to work on our behalf.

When I was studying classical ballet and I was going for my exam, I had to have both legs be able to go as high as each other in arabesque in order to achieve a good pass. A few days before my exam my left leg was at 120 degrees, but for some reason my right leg was only at 80 degrees. I couldn't get my right leg to go as high as my left.

As part of my training I used visualisation, and each night I would run through my dance in my imagination before I went to sleep. I began to imagine that my right leg was light as a feather and easy to control, and that it was attached to my fingertips so that I could raise it up. It sounds a bit out-there, but I immersed myself in the feeling of lightness and ease.

One day the principal came in to observe the major

students and I knew she was assessing me in preparation for the exam. I stayed with that feeling of lightness and I raised my left leg first, lowered it, and then my right leg, and my right leg went as high as my left. They matched. It was so easy I couldn't believe it.

After a time, I realised that I was allowing my subconscious mind to sabotage my success in the upcoming exam. But, without realising what I was really doing back then, I had overcome my belief by visualising a new set of behaviours. Not only that, but I had begun to focus on what I really wanted, what was for my highest good. Passing that exam so that I could teach classical ballet at that point was for my highest good.

And it's not just me. I can tell you of many examples when this has happened.

Dr David Hamilton has studied the mind-body connection, and in his article, 'Visualisation Alters the Brain and Body,'[8] he states: 'Your brain cannot tell the difference between something that's real or whether you are just imagining it.'

He refers to an experiment done by Harvard scientists involving brain scans and imagery. The scientists taught a simple five-fingered combination of piano notes to a group of people, which they practised playing for two hours a day, over five consecutive days. Another group of volunteers were given the same notes but didn't in fact play them; they just imagined playing them. They visualised playing the same combination for the same time period, two hours a day for five consecutive days.

Dr Hamilton says that the brain scans for the volunteers who actually did the physical practising and the ones who imagined playing the notes were the same. The brain, he says, can't tell the difference between what's real and what's imagined.

When we practise visualisation techniques we create positive impressions on our subconscious to manifest our dreams. I have used these techniques many times and they have been successful. You have to really believe and concentrate on what you want, and if it is for your highest good and will not harm yourself or others, then it can and will happen.

Also known as mental imagery or mental rehearsal, visualisation is a powerful tool for practising when you can't physically practise. Visualisation has been used by sports psychologists to improve athletic performance, competitive edge, mental awareness, wellbeing and confidence. It is also used by musicians and dancers to rehearse. According to Dr Sarah McKay from The Neuroscience Academy,[9] it's thought that when performed appropriately, mental rehearsal activates the same motor, somatosensory, auditory and emotional circuits as the actual physical act. In other words, imagined practise may activate the same neural circuits as real experience.

For years as a dancer and dance teacher I practised visualisation when 'marking out' the dance in the class and when practising in my mind when I wasn't physically able to dance something out fully. Dancers basically rehearse in their mind every day, living out the whole experience: the kinaesthetic response, hearing the music, imagining feeling the floor, the range of movement, the dynamics, expression and artistry. As a classical dancer, practising this way was a daily occurrence for me and it overcame any lack of confidence and kept the performance in the forefront of my mind.

But you don't need to be an athlete or performer to harness the power of visualisation. Anyone can rehearse how to respond emotionally to an event.

There are two types of mental imagery:
- Internal imagery, also known as kinaesthetic or first-person imagery, where you visualise yourself doing the activity
- External imagery, or third person imagery, where you visualise doing the activity from the perspective of an onlooker

Internal imagery is more powerful than external imagery and generates significantly more physiological responses, such as changes in heart rate, blood pressure and respiration rate.

To be effective, mental rehearsal needs to be developed and practised regularly. There are four key elements: relaxation, realism (first person, involving all senses, actions, thoughts and emotions), regularity and reinforcement. So:
- create the basic picture
- add the sensory details
- refine the script
- rehearse for short periods every day.

Prepare your subconscious

When you concentrate and impress what you want on your subconscious mind, information and circumstances start to support you in achieving your goals. You may be given an opportunity that will lead to what you want. Be open to this. It's a matter of seeing through the mist of your own filters to what is possible. Twenty years ago, I created a vision board in a scrapbook. My vision board had the following pictures: A comfortable home with a living area that had white walls and wooden floors; two daughters playing happily in the courtyard; a husband with a crisp white shirt and silver hair looking in the same direction as me; me sitting on the chairs in the courtyard and coaching.

When I open my scrapbook and see what I had on my vision board, it is absolutely amazing. I can't believe I have achieved what I set out to create so long ago.

You can use this same visualisation technique to achieve your deepest desires.

- Create a vision board. You can do this on cardboard, in a scrapbook, on a corkboard or as an electronic document. Use pictures that show what you most deeply desire.
- Pick a word or affirmation associated with these desires and write it in your diary each week.
- Meditate on what you want to create.

One thing I learnt from looking back at my vision board was that the ability to manifest what we want is a function of what we feel we deserve. This can tap into our sense of unworthiness. If we feel we only deserve so much, then no matter how hard or how many times we say we want more, chances are it won't happen. When I created my vision board I didn't think I deserved these things. I needed to learn to say 'yes' to what I wanted, to believe it was possible and that I did deserve it. Only then did it become a reality.

If we feel we only deserve so much then no matter how hard or how many times we say we want more, chances are it won't happen.

When you take the steps to get out of your perceived comfort zone and into your true comfort zone it really does require you to be honest about what you want and to have the courage to ask for it. This is important, because if those around you aren't aware of your needs, they can't help you and may unintentionally block your progress. It can be scary, but as the spiritual leader Emmet Fox said, 'Do it trembling if you must, but do it.'[10]

It's okay just to ask and be heard. The important thing here is to be able to identify what it is you need and then to ask for it. You may not always get what you want. If the timing isn't right or that person can't give it to you, then you can take the steps to address that need in some other way. Take the time to think about what you really want, write it down, put it in an envelope and put it away somewhere special. Put a date on it and take it out in a year's time and notice what has happened.

CASE STUDY

When my clients come to see me, I often start by asking what is it that they want. Sometimes they say they don't know what they want and sometimes they say they want what everyone else is wanting. They have become lost in the maze of demands of others or they reach a point where they actually don't know what they want anymore.

One particular client came to see me feeling completely overwhelmed. He had a challenging job and lots of competing demands, both in and out of work. He had a presentation for work that he needed to prepare, he wanted to watch his son in a debating team, his wife wanted to arrange a date night, and he hadn't exercised in three weeks.

When I looked at him, I could see that his shoulders were raised, his breathing was shallow, his face was slightly red and he seemed quite anxious.

'What would you like?' I asked him. 'If you could have anything right now, what would it be?'

Well, obviously a holiday would have been great for him, but he realised that he had lost himself in what was expected of him.

It was a relief for him to even be asked this question. He said he hadn't thought about it for a long time. So we teased out his imaginings and, most importantly, identified what he wanted amidst all that was going on. He realised he was trying to please everyone and his frustration was that he just needed to stop and take some time for himself.

His presentation was important, so he asked his family to allow him the privacy to complete it that evening. That way he could attend a debating afternoon for his son and lock in a date with his wife in a fortnight.

My client's goal was to put himself first for a month and to reassess how this change in perspective would impact his life and responsibilities. He needed to focus on taking care of himself first so that he would have the energy needed to be good for others. He needed to be courageous enough to ask for what he wanted and needed. This changed the balance in the relationship and it was for the betterment of everyone.

I heard a quote the other day from Oprah Winfrey and it really resonated with me: 'You can have it all but just not all at once.' I thought how relevant that was in my life as I had been expecting to have everything all at once and exhausting myself trying to make it happen.

Look at what you want, set up a plan and be patient because it may take a little longer than you think. You can and will have what you want eventually.

CHAPTER 6

Procrastination

You've taken some baby steps out of your perceived comfort zone, identified your boundaries, identified what you truly want in life, visualised it, now you're ready to step into your true comfort zone.

When you get into your true comfort zone you:

- embrace change
- achieve goals
- try new things
- meet new people
- accept your limitations; accept where you are right now (once you do that, you can move to the next stage from this baseline)
- accept your beliefs (do this with love – reframe them to support you)

- aim higher (trust your higher power)
- stay motivated (know what your true motivation is and go with it)
- align your life with your higher purpose
- quietly and confidently trust yourself.

Sounds good, doesn't it? So what's holding you back? What's stopping you from doing what you know is true and right for you in your life?

As I have told you, many years ago I started writing a book on procrastination – or rather, overcoming procrastination – and I was procrastinating and couldn't finish it. Now that you have discovered what you truly want, what is truly right for you, this is when you might just start to experience procrastination, so it's important to understand it and learn to manage it.

Procrastination is delaying or putting off until tomorrow what you know you need to be doing today – postponing an action that you need to take. Each baby step you take to step out of your perceived comfort zone and reach your true comfort zone can be an opportunity for you to procrastinate. When you accept the boundaries and value your perceived comfort zone, you are more likely to take the next steps with compassion and true conviction.

Not only will procrastination impede your progress towards your true comfort zone, it can be devastating in both your personal and professional life. If left unchecked, procrastination can lead to further procrastination, especially if you are justifying the behaviour and reinforcing it. Continued procrastination may cause guilt, severe loss of personal effectiveness leading to disapproval for not meeting commitments, and stress. Long-term it can affect your self-esteem. You know you are ultimately letting yourself down. You know you should be doing the thing and you are cheating yourself of the best opportunity. So it is important for your total wellbeing to be able to recognise the first signs that you are procrastinating, nip it in the bud and commit to staying in charge of your life. In short, pushing out of your perceived comfort zone does not work nearly as effectively as accepting where you are and taking considered steps to align to your higher self.

You must learn to raise the value of certain priorities even if you don't necessarily want to do them. When you value a task, or you value yourself enough then you are more likely to complete it. Reframing the action or perception of it can assist you to move forward.

Psychologist and hypnotherapist Andrew Dobson says that in the general population the predominant reason people procrastinate is a breakdown in self-control – you know what you ought to do and you're not able to bring yourself to do it. It's that gap, he says, between intention and action.[11]

It is critical to understand that justifying putting things off serves a very important purpose – it allows us to continue to procrastinate by minimising the perceived effects of our actions and allowing us to continue to feel good about who we are.

Your understanding of the ways in which you minimise and excuse your lack of taking action is important, so that you can identify the process and consciously challenge your feelings and behaviour.

One of my mentors once said to me that I had a case of 'excusitis', that I was making excuses and that the book of excuses was all the same. Well, that burst my bubble. I thought that I was pretty creative at inventing reasons for not doing something. It's easy to say:

- 'I don't have time.'
- 'I'm too old.'
- 'I'm too young.'
- 'I'm not educated enough.'

If you are truly honest, it's just that for a time you are afraid to step forward. When you think about what the benefits might be and stay focused on them, then the fear starts to dissipate. For example, what will public speaking do for your career and your personal growth?

Individuals procrastinate when they disconnect from their innate ability to accomplish what they have decided to do. They put off or postpone action because they believe that they are not ready yet or unprepared. They forfeit their ability to overcome life's challenges and to do what they know is true and right for them.

Procrastination occurs when you have lost your courage and start to feel weak, when you forget to keep following your heart. 'Motivation' comes from the Latin verb *'movere'*, which means to move. If you do not move or take action, then your energy will cease to flow. When you add your will to action, power begins to flow and your creative juices are once again realised.

When you postpone action then your inner talents and gifts are not only suppressed, you end up suffering. I believe the two greatest powers in life are loving and doing what you want to do. When you let yourself down and don't persevere, push ahead and back your heart, then you will suffer the pain of not being true to yourself and the regret of unrealised potential. You end up reinforcing and reinstating this negative or fixed mindset. In a sense it becomes stronger.

A way to overcome procrastination is to acknowledge your feelings. When you can fully feel your passion, procrastination dissipates. By getting out of your head and coming from your passion, you don't think about it, you just feel it and do it.

By being aware that you are analysing the logical (head) versus coming from your feeling state, desire or passion (heart) you stop thinking about pros and cons and just do what really is in your best interest. When you tap into your higher purpose, then it simplifies the process and you just get on with it without the anxiety.

Accountability is the key. When you sign a contract with yourself, you wholeheartedly invest in you. This commitment or pledge you make with yourself is not negotiable, and when you follow through you build your self-esteem and confidence.

Each baby step you take to step out of your perceived comfort zone and reach your true comfort zone can be an opportunity for you to procrastinate.

Do you procrastinate?

In my experience the thing we most want is the thing

we most procrastinate on. Why? Because quite often it is so important to us that the very doing of it raises our doubts and fears. This is the fundamental reason why we put off what we know we should do for our greater good. We play games, but they are only games with ourselves and we are losing valuable time, energy and money, which cannot be reclaimed.

Well, you are not alone. Procrastination prevails with the best and the worst of us and it's all due to what we believe about ourselves. We need to look past the obvious and look to the end game. So with that in mind, let's begin.

You think you are an action-taking person? Try this quick quiz. Recognise if you are procrastinating, as some people don't even know they are doing it.

- Do you leave the exam preparation to the last minute?
- Do you put off doing the presentation hoping you can wing it on the day?
- Do you spend time on activities that derail you from your goal?
- Do you distract yourself – look at Facebook, phone a friend to talk about the fact that you have stuff to do?
- Do you do just about anything to avoid the most

important task in your day, rather than sit down and actually do it?
- Do you tell yourself that it will all be okay because you are thinking about it?
- Do you hover at the coffee machine? Doodle at your desk?
- Do you find yourself with the cleanest home, having downed numerous cups of coffee, only to realise that you still haven't done what you promised yourself you would do?

The list is endless!

If you are still not sure if you are procrastinating, look for these signs and symptoms:

1. Signs of procrastination

Here are some telltale signs that you may be procrastinating. See if you identify with any of the following: poor presentation, eating more, drinking more than usual, increased coffee intake, increased sugar intake, sleeping more or less than usual, work piling up on your desk, missing appointments, avoiding completing tasks, avoiding making phone calls, blaming others, blaming yourself, a constantly full inbox, writing and rewriting the same to-do list.

How busy are you really? How busy do you look? Are you being productive? Are you busy or productive?

2. Symptoms of procrastination

What are you feeling?

Anxious, overwhelmed, not sleeping, teary, unfocused, clouded judgement, fearful, stressed, neck pain, headaches, back pain, everything is an effort?

Procrastination leaves you feeling overwhelmed. You can rush around stressing yourself, dumping and blaming others for not bending to your last-minute wishes. If you are lucky you end up winging it. It may work or your lack of preparation may mean you don't do so well.

Either way you are doing yourself a disservice. Procrastination has raised its ugly head and prevented you realising your full potential.

Overcoming procrastination

Author and motivational speaker Mel Robbins has discovered what she calls the five-second rule.[12] Applying this rule will help you to stop procrastinating and start taking action, start taking steps. Mel Robbins found that the moment you feel like acting on a goal you have only five seconds to physically move or your brain will stop you. Five seconds! That's not long. One way to help you take action is to prepare yourself – to get ready ahead of time so that it's easy to move within five seconds.

In winter it feels too cold to go for a morning walk. It's easy to wake up, think about going, but stay snuggled up in bed until it is too late to go. How to overcome this? I decided to apply Mel's five-second rule. I prepared for the next day so that I could act quickly. I wore my tracksuit to bed and had my shoes at the base of the bed. As soon as I woke up I got out of bed and put my shoes on. I was out of the door before my head could stop me. If I hadn't prepared for action, I know I would have said, 'It's too cold, I'll go tonight,' and hibernated like a bear.

I beat myself at my own game and soon got into the habit. I realised the benefits and now I miss my walk if I don't go.

Keep the end game in mind

You have to do a presentation with a view to going for a promotion. You are not keen on presenting and fear that you may not do well.

Q: Why are you doing the presentation?
A: To go for a promotion.
Q: What will that mean to you?
A: More money.

Q: If you have that what will that mean to you?
A: More prestige.

Q: If you have that what will the result be?
A: Recognised by colleagues and my partner will be proud of me.

Q: What will it mean to you if you have all of that?
A: It means that I can plan a holiday and spend some quality time with my children, instead of working long hours for little return and feeling too tired to play with them when I get home.

Now, what is the real end game here, you may ask? The end game is quality time with the children. In other words, being a present and proud parent.

This is a common example that I have heard from many of my clients. Being recognised and proud is what motivates them to get that original presentation done. Having time with family is what truly motivates them.

I've found as a coach and through my own personal experience, it's not about the immediate, it's about what it will ultimately give you. What are you really doing all this for? What is your end game? This is the gold.

AN EXERCISE

Think of one thing you are procrastinating on right now – one step you want to take out of your perceived comfort zone and towards your true comfort zone. Every time you put it off, stop and pause while you take a big breath and think.

How does it feel?

Ask yourself: What is it costing me if I don't do this? What will it mean to me if I do get it done? If I get it done what will the result be?

Keep asking until you have the answers.

Then ask: If all of this is in place what will it mean to me personally?

This answer is your end game: your real motivation. Remember how I talked about baby steps? Now take one small step towards your end game. If we go back to my earlier example, that could mean preparing the outline for the presentation or talking to someone about it. Your mindset matters.

To help you get more clarity about your end game, I'd like you to consider these questions:

What is it that you really want?

When you look back a year from now and you have achieved this goal, who did you need to be?

What did you need to have in place?

What did you need to do both personally and professionally to get the results and success you achieved?

Write these things down as if you have already attained your goal. It's up to you to do the things you need to do.

I'll use myself as an example.

Who did I need to be? I needed to believe in myself, have the courage of my own convictions, be brave enough to speak up about my dreams and aspirations and be determined and focused.

What did I need to have in place? I needed to ask for help from those who had done what I wanted to do. As well, I needed to have a certain amount of income to cover the cost of being able to take myself to the next level and not worry financially, which would have undermined my confidence.

What did I need to do personally? I needed to keep fit and healthy, to work on my mindset so that I remained positive when the going got tough. I needed to enlist support from my colleagues and family, and I needed to not go on a fancy holiday until I had achieved my goal.

What did I need to do professionally? I needed to sign up for a course on speaking professionally and enlist an editor.

It worked! Clarity cleared the procrastination for me. I now knew what I needed to do in order to succeed and reach my goal.

The *why*

Developing your own *why* is paramount to how you grow. What is your vision and, more importantly, what is your mission statement of why you are stepping out of your perceived comfort zone and into your true comfort zone?

When you look beyond your current situation, your thinking goes to a higher level. For example, my vision is of me standing at the airport smiling as my book is being displayed as a best seller! My mission is to make use of all of the creativity I have in me to assist others in achieving their true comfort zone. This is my *why*. If I achieve my mission, I would feel satisfied that I had done what I am meant to do.

Go back to this process when you feel anxious or fearful. Then you will be able to overcome the limited thinking and expand on your mission.

As author and speaker Simon Sinek says, 'The WHY is the purpose, cause or belief that drives every one of us.'[13] This becomes your most empowering vehicle to success.

The roles we play

We all have roles that we step into as a way to justify our procrastination. Identifying and acknowledging them makes it easier for us to overcome our inertia.

I've developed a list of some of the roles. Have fun identifying and acknowledging the ones you play.

Olly Overwhelm
This can be when your goal is too big, or you simply don't know how to do it, or are afraid you may not do it well enough – perfectionism – so you delay finishing until it is perfect. Unfortunately, this kind of perfection is an illusion. Just start. Ninety percent may be good enough to the outside world compared to your own expectations of 100 percent.

Cleaning Clara
Whilst working from home I realise I have to answer all of my emails. Suddenly, the house couldn't be cleaner. Even the fridge gets cleaned out! When that happens, I know I'm procrastinating. It's a matter of taking myself up to the office, sitting my butt in the chair and just doing it!

Put-it-off Pete
It could be that you have to make that long overdue call and find that you go for a coffee two or three times under the guise of having a break or a breather.

Stay-in-bed Fred
You keep turning the alarm to snooze or turning it off completely, assuring yourself for the fifth time that you will go for a run tomorrow. But tomorrow becomes the busiest day of the week!

Social media Sally
You feel compelled to look at Facebook, LinkedIn or Instagram to see who is successful, rather than doing what will enhance your own success. Suddenly social media has become your priority.

Busy Betty
You distract yourself with seemingly important things rather than focusing on what you have to do. Organising social events, tidying the office, catching up with colleagues having a few jokes. Doing anything and everything rather than the task at hand.

Which games do you play? What's your unique procrastination style?

Reframe your thinking
Psychology tells us that whatever we associate with pain we will avoid, and whatever we associate with pleasure we will be drawn towards.

So when we make decisions, it's not what we think, it's what we feel about the decision that really matters. This means that when we are deciding whether or not to do something, we have to be honest about our feelings. And sometimes we just have to force ourselves to do it.

It's also interesting to note that the size of the task will expand to the amount of time given to it. A task could only need ten hours to complete, but because you have four days to get it done, it can take many more hours. Why aren't you getting it done sooner than later? Because you attach pain to working on the task and are more comfortable delaying it.

To get the task done it helps to reframe your thinking about it. You need to focus on the positive feelings associated with finishing it, rather than the painful feelings associated with working on it.

AN EXERCISE

Think about your goal. Keep it simple.

Where are you on a scale of one to ten with ten being the greatest?

What does it feel like? Look like? Smell, sound, and taste like?

What is in the gap between where you are and ten? What do

you need to do to succeed? What do you need to do, be or have in place to make it a ten?

Reframe your thinking – what are the benefits of taking action and getting it done?

List ten benefits.

What are the benefits of not achieving your goal?

If you are like me, it is easy to stay in your perceived comfort zone – to stay with a sense of anticipation and prevent the risk of failure or criticism or judgement. List the consequences for you of not getting it done.

What is the cost benefit of getting it done sooner than later?

What do you gain?

You don't decide to procrastinate it just happens, and then hours later you realise you have accomplished little towards your end game. You need to reframe your thinking and focus on how good it will feel when you get it done.

Ten tips to get it done:

- Tell others what your intention is.
- Set aside distractions, phone calls and interruptions.
- Cement the positive motivation necessary to complete the task.
- Do one thing at a time and finish it.

- Step back and take a strategic view.
- Enlist help – off-load what you don't like doing or can't do quickly.
- Focus on what you do best.
- Solve the problems.
- Find the best place to start.
- Go for a walk and clear your head.

What are you focusing on now?

We are being constantly distracted from what we want.

As a coach, I take my clients through a process to understand what they really want and what really drives them. I'm amazed at how many individuals do not know or don't take the time to identify this. They get on a treadmill or on automatic pilot, bouncing through their day doing what others want or is expected of them.

Most say, 'I don't know what I want', 'I can't ever have it anyway', 'How could I have this?' Some immediately fall into self-doubt, whilst others ask, 'Can I truly have what I want?'

When you look at what you want with a laser-beam focus and intention, then you will start to see it all around you. Have you ever focused on the red Mini Cooper you wanted and found that for the next week that it is all you saw? Well, it's the same for anything in our lives. What you focus on you will get more of. So be careful.

What are you actually focusing on now? Rather than focusing on debt, focus instead on a savings plan to be debt-free. It is so subtle yet so effective when we know how.

You see, it is about how you are thinking about what you want.

- How committed are you to achieving it?
- Are you allowing distractions to interfere?
- Are you allowing others to sway you?

One of my client's goals was to get a promotion. After exploring his self-doubt and enlisting confidence and strategies to support him, he not only was successful at the interview but the company created an even better position for him to further his career. He consulted with me to identify what was blocking him internally and externally, focused on what he wanted – better pay and prestige – and took action to make it happen, and ended up with more than he thought he deserved.

You must focus on the result you want to achieve. Then and only then will you get the results. Take time out to invest in you. Get off the treadmill and identify your outcome and what it will give you.

Taking the time to define what you want and taking charge of making it happen is the first step. Be practical regarding goals and set yourself up to get things done, especially if it means asking for help. Remind yourself that everyone has difficulties and challenges – it will hold you in good stead. And most importantly, stay focused on what you want.

AN EXERCISE

Close your eyes. Focus on the colour Red Red Red. Now open your eyes. What are you seeing when you look around the room? How much red is there?

What you are focusing on is like a search engine. If you are focused on red Mini Coopers, you will see them everywhere. You create much of your world by what you choose to focus on.

Five ways to stay focused:

- Take time to quietly decide what you want.
- Write it down and refer to it every day.
- Enlist a coach if you have doubts and beliefs blocking you from achieving what you want.
- Put distractions and negativity aside.
- Keep it small and achievable until you get the confidence that it works.

If you believe it then you will see it.

Confidence

Confidence is the top of the list of must-haves for every client I have ever worked with. At some point in the sessions the issue of self-confidence always emerges.

Sometimes clients feel that the lack of confidence is at the root of all their problems, while for others it may affect only one area of their life. I want you to know that we all have different levels of confidence and that many people lack confidence, it's just that some people are better at hiding it than others.

It is not possible to feel confident all the time. It's important and helpful to know this as it lets you off the hook and creates a more realistic approach to life. So now you can stop expecting yourself to be a perfectly composed and confident person who is full of self-assurance twenty-four hours a day. This person cannot exist. Part of being human means that we do hold ourselves back with our doubts and self-critical thoughts, which can block our path to success.

If you take the view of being an opportunist, you will create new openings and possibilities for yourself. It's like a door opening to a fresh and exciting new area of your life every step you take. If you visualise knocking on a new door, you might feel nervous and full of trepidation as it opens. However, when you visualise stepping through that door and embracing that opportunity or challenge, you may find it is not as daunting as if you were to keep holding yourself back. This is a great strategy when you are on the brink of new challenges.

Invest in you and live your life to the full. Step forward, be noticed, grab chances and expect a fulfilled life. Even when you are nervous act 'as if'. When you radiate confidence, you show the world that you believe in yourself, but more importantly that you have the courage of your own convictions. People pick up on this energy. Be vibrant, charismatic and show that you respect and support yourself with your ideas and opinions. At an unconscious level people will be attracted to you and the cycle begins.

Many of my clients say, 'I want to wait till I have confidence' or 'I don't feel confident enough'. In that case, you need to take steps to build your confidence. Remember learning to ride a bike as a child? Someone helped you get on, encouraged you until you could steady yourself, until you could push yourself and balance, steer it in the right direction and take off. Well, it's the same with everything you do. You get the confidence when you have a go!

Don't wait for your confidence to grow before you

step out of your fortress, which is your perceived comfort zone. Take the step now. Even if it is tiny, it is better than no step at all.

Taking a step, having a go, builds your confidence. But more importantly, it changes your mindset about who you are being in that moment, what you can actually do. You might go for it and fail but you took the chance, you made the choice to try. That in itself starts to build and sustain your confidence.

You learn to be confident, it doesn't just happen.

Managing the little monkey on your shoulder

There is a little monkey on our shoulder that, we all have, one who tells us all the ways to doubt ourselves. A little monkey who says it won't work, and uses scare tactics to keep us paralysed in our thinking.

Changing these negative beliefs is imperative to your emotional growth and business development. Most highly successful people – Steve Jobs, Richard Branson, Bill Gates – have gone through challenges about whether their vision will succeed.

When you manage the inner critic, or the monkey on your shoulder, you are then able to separate yourself from outside negative criticisms and judgements. You become more of who you are, and you are able to give yourself validation and positive feedback rather than rely on external forces. Once you recognise that this voice has no power over you, you can step into a new state of confidence.

Common beliefs that hold us back are:
- I'm not good enough
- I can't do this
- I don't deserve this much
- I don't matter.

We need to catch ourselves when we hear ourselves think or say these statements as they come from our own inner critic, and it can be quite powerful. We can project this belief onto our outer world and create situations to validate and prove ourselves right. Therefore, it is imperative to master your perception of this chatter.

As a confident person you will focus on your goal. You will live, eat and breathe what you want connected to your passion; you'll be unafraid to take a risk; and you'll steadfastly pursue your actions daily.

Here are some tips to increase your confidence:
- Know that you are special; there is no one else like you.
- Stand tall and smile.

- Breathe.
- Expect the best.
- Get out there and get noticed.
- Surround yourself with positive people who support you and your dreams.
- Laugh – it's sometimes hilarious what we do to ourselves.
- Clear the clutter.
- Back yourself more when the going gets tough.
- Reward yourself and celebrate your success.
- Exercise daily.
- Allocate time for you.
- Focus on your strengths and talents.

Confident people are like a champagne glass overflowing with the fullness of life. They project experience, enthusiasm and expectation. They welcome challenges and the thrill of riding it out. They recognise they are learning the lessons of life, and the quicker they learn the more successful they will be. Hence, when you get on the wave and ride it, you land on the shore of success. This takes trust, self-belief, the ability to let go, and a belief that the universe is supporting you for your highest good.

When you are able to find meaning in the disappointments and failures this strengthens your confidence, giving you new reserves that you can call on when you are in need.

Confidence is your reward when you invest in you and overcome your fear. When you know who you really are, can focus, stay centred and adjust to the ever-changing outer world. When you can roll with the punches and still believe you are on track, then confidence is yours and your true comfort zone is within your grasp.

If one advances confidently in the direction of his dreams, and endeavours to live the life which he has imagined, he will meet with a success unexpected in common hours.[14]

Henry David Thoreau

CHAPTER 7

What do you really want?

Have you ever had that moment when you've wanted to speak up at a meeting with a great innovative idea but you held yourself back only to hear your colleague push forward and say what you were going to suggest? Don't you just hate that!

What happened? Did you contract and hold yourself back? Did you feel self-conscious, afraid of what others might think? Didn't want to step into the limelight and become the centre of attention? Then you heard someone else state exactly what your ingenious idea was, and furthermore take all of the credit for it.

Yes, you ignored your natural genius. This is your natural genius. And in that moment, it is lost to the one who has the loudest voice and can sell your idea.

Here's the thing: you think you are comfortable in your perceived comfort zone. You pretend you don't mind and give up graciously to another. But you are denying your right to tell the world your idea. What you believe will work. It's yours!

This is your natural genius. So, step into that true comfort zone and own it. It's your idea, so get into the flow of it, trust it. That flow you experience is timeless and effortless; it is where all creativity is born. Flow is when the hours go by and you don't even realise you've missed a meal and are totally in the zone.

This is stepping into your true comfort zone.

Stay true to yourself

If you make a decision and things don't turn out, you can still process your feelings and come back to the self. When you process your feelings of disappointment and discouragement you will gain power.

If you stay on the fence and you do not commit or make a decision, you can end up disconnecting from your true self, your true comfort zone. You can end up letting yourself down, your self-esteem drops and then you feel weaker.

It is okay to change course, have the courage to do so

and follow your heart. While in the process of moving towards what you think is true and right for you, you are still connected to your inner self, which is strong, persistent, directed, purposeful and quietly confident.

We each have our own inner authority where we can access our own best answers. It's very resourceful and I usually get some great answers through that process. I feel empowered and can tap into my own wisdom. I'm in charge of my care. How do I sustain myself in each and every moment?

When you continue to invest in you in each area of your life, you enrich yourself holistically. Remind yourself to fill up in each area of your life because as you start to fill up in one it will then overflow into the other areas. Being healthy and fit, for example, will cause you to feel positive and energised and that will help to keep you balanced at work and in your relationship. When you address a career matter then your focus and confidence will rise, improving your ability to manage yourself and others.

Another reason people put off going for what they want is that they think they are not ready. They believe if they were ready that they would have no fears, worries or anxieties. This is not true. You can often have some trepidation. When you get started then the fears will gradually diminish and your courage and confidence will start to grow.

When you get what you think you want, is it what you really want?

This is an interesting question because it brings to mind what your end game is. It helps to clarify what you are really here for. What you really want will supersede what you think you want.

You see, sometimes we go down a path thinking it's the right one, and then as time goes on we get a few messages that perhaps it's not in our best interest.

CASE STUDY

One of my clients, Veronica, was the CEO of a large government organisation and she felt she wanted to do something more meaningful.

Together we worked on her definition of meaningfulness and she decided to apply for a role in more of a volunteer capacity in a charitable organisation. And yes, she got it. But after six months she realised that she wanted to be able to have more autonomy, more of a challenge and to exercise her creativity. She wasn't feeling fulfilled at this level. She wasn't able to express herself to her full capacity.

It became apparent that she would have to tell the people

she worked with and she found this to be a devastating thought. She had believed that this was what she wanted to do. Also, she didn't want to let her colleagues down.

Veronica went through a series of processes to come to terms with the fact that it was all right to change her mind. You see she knew what she wanted, but she initially didn't have the courage to go for it. Consequently, she then had to find the courage to change her mind and follow her conviction, her heart. She had to acknowledge that if she continued with the original decision it wasn't going to work, because that goal wasn't aligned with her true comfort zone, what she knew would be ultimately true and right for her.

It was okay for her to change her mind because it wasn't really a mistake; it was a step in the right direction. It meant that she was able to take her time, reassess and find her true comfort zone – fulfilled, challenged, creative, able to motivate others and execute her talents fully.

Action strengthens our belief and is what attracts success.

Intentions

An intention is a determination or resolution to do something. You determine in your mind that you are going to take some action or achieve some goal.

By setting your intentions at the beginning of each day you start to experience that great feeling when the world responds to your desires. Not only are you more successful, you don't have to try and do so much.

Confidence that we can do something is trusting that our intended outcome will happen. Whatever we do, we are really just telling our mind, body and heart what to do. What makes it happen is the connection to the true self and a clear awareness of what we want. Practise gives us confidence. Confidence and intention results in success.

> *In our quiet moments we all know what is true and right for us.*

Get in touch with what you really want

When I started playing golf I was very tense in my shoulders as I was trying so hard to make my ball go a longer distance. Being an amateur and having a small build, I only have the strength for a shorter distance. The aim at the end of the day is to have the ball go straight and in the right direction. Once I let go of the expectation I had on myself I could relax and visualise the ball landing on the green in three swings rather than in one like my male friends.

I visualised the relaxed swing of my arms, and heard

in my mind the sound of the ball hitting the club head just at the right moment. If you're a golfer, you'll know the unique sound when you can tell you have hit it on the mark. And I visualised the ball flowing through the air low and straight and landing on the putting green.

You see, we have so much power in our thinking and our imagination but we rarely tap into it. In fact, as I'm writing this, it's reminded me now to revisit this process of visualisation on a daily basis and put it into a regular practice, a more conscious one.

When I used visualisation to improve my golf swing, at one level what I wanted was to get the ball to the putting green in one shot. But at a deeper level what I really wanted was to overcome my anxiety about my golf swing and just enjoy playing.

It was the same when I used visualisation for my major dance exam. At one level I wanted to pass the exam with flying colours, but at another level what I really wanted was to master my fear of success and enjoy dancing!

If I passed my exam, then what? I really love to dance. For me it's the lifeblood of my soul to hear a piece of music and respond, create and move to it. It gives me sheer delight. It taps into my soul.

When I get what I want (to pass the exam) what is it

that I really want (to feel the freedom of accomplishment, the lightness and flow of moving to music, the energy, creativity and passion that emanates from my body)? I could go on. It's a sense of completeness, of being at one with the universe, connected at another whole level, knowing, trusting that this is true and right for me.

As I am typing this, I realise that my ability to type is learnt but my fingers move without thinking and at a great speed. Again, it just flows. This is what I call 'getting into your true comfort zone', where time just goes, you don't feel hunger, you don't feel thirst, you're totally immersed in the moment and it's all just happening.

It's the same with golf. You are on the greens, air on your face, at one with nature and you are balanced and relaxed. It's an easy swing back and the energy just flows from your mind down your arm, into the wrist, the grip, the iron, and connects with the point where you hear the sound. You know you have hit it right, the angle is perfectly positioned and the ball is in the sky almost still, poised, and then you see it land on the green. Golfers, you know what I mean.

When you get what you want, what is it that you really want? For golf, what you really want can be that sense of satisfaction, achievement, overcoming the challenge, nailing the ball at the right angle, overcoming the weather and knowing that sense of freedom and achievement.

Getting in touch with what you really want is the key to success. It surpasses the obvious, the immediate. It's the essence of who you are, and we need to constantly remind ourselves of what that is and express that part.

Acceptance

Acceptance can transform the way you experience life. Acceptance is about letting go of the old that isn't serving you anymore. Taking the filters off of how you think your life should be and seeing it as it is and can be.

Quite often our filters are stopping us from having what we truly deserve. Notice who is coming into your life and who is moving away. What opportunities are you not noticing or saying 'no' to? No judgement about this, simply notice. Notice who you are being in the world as you begin to set yourself free. Practise being fully present to this.

I did an exercise in a workshop once and asked the team to act as if they were being this confident new character in a new role, and we had so much fun with it. I couldn't believe some of the transformations that occurred in that twenty-minute exercise.

The participants didn't believe they had it in them. But guess what, they did. It begs the question, if it is in us all then why don't we just call on that self and make it purposeful? Have fun with that!

When you accept that there may be so much more in store for you, and trust that your higher power is presenting so much more to you, then you can experience life with more peace of mind.

Kathy Caprino, in an article for *Forbes*,[15] wrote that as a women's career coach and leadership developer she'd noticed that one of the most harmful things you can do to your career is to remain in a role where you are comfortable for years and years. Not only do you start to doubt your value to other employers, you also begin to wonder if you have what it takes to succeed in any other role. She learnt the hard way that no job is secure. There is only one thing in this life that is secure, she says, and that is you – your essence, your energy, your gifts and talents, and your ability to make a difference when something really matters to you. It's what I call your natural genius, your true self, your true comfort zone. Learn from these insights. Step out of your perceived comfort zone and into your true comfort zone. This is what will give you certainty; it surpasses all else.

Inspire others

Others notice what you do, whether you realise it or not. You can be a role model. What you do can inspire others to grow and change. This applies not only at work, but also at home, setting an example for your children. We all have a teacher or someone in our lives who unknowingly inspired and motivated us to do more than we thought we could. Taking risks and believing in yourself allows you to be that person for others. You will have no regrets at the end.

As a coach, one question I have asked of myself and one that I ask my clients is: What would you like to have said at your eulogy? In other words, how would you like to be remembered?

For most of us, the answer isn't about the material things that we leave or the goals that we have achieved, but the love that we have left behind. Perhaps a kind word when someone was down, perhaps a word of encouragement, perhaps being with someone when they needed an ear. These are the things that stand the test of time, that are remembered when you touch the heart of another.

Who you are is what you will be remembered for.

CHAPTER 8

Who are you?

The transformation zone is where we give ourselves permission to be who we truly are. But most of us hold back, like I did at the networking function when I didn't go up and introduce myself to the woman I wanted to meet. However, we do have a choice. So I ask you: Do you stay protecting yourself in your fort? Stand at the door of opportunity and crumble in doubt? Or do you step into your forté, what I call your 'true comfort zone', quietly and confidently standing in your power?

This is where you need to give yourself permission to step into your true comfort zone, to follow through and to trust. This can be the most challenging step as you are about to step out and announce yourself. Make sure that you have everything in place so that you are confident.

By this stage in the process, you have acknowledged that you needed to make a change in your perceived comfort zone and have addressed your doubts with compassion. In your uncomfortable zone you have had the courage to identify the beliefs that don't serve you anymore and replaced them with encouraging ones. You have become comfortable with being uncomfortable, knowing that this is just part of the learning. You now realise that you have a choice and can take charge and create your life based on your true comfort zone. You have become clear about who you are in your clarity zone and accepted that you can transform the way you experience life. Now it's about taking personal responsibility for your own freedom and fulfillment.

'Responsibility' is a curious word. It has two shorter words in it: 'response' and 'ability'. When we think about responsibility, the word can weigh heavily on our hearts as it can mean having to fulfil a duty that we may or may not want to do. When you turn the word into 'the ability to respond' it becomes more empowering.

As you transform, how will you respond to outside comments, both positive and negative? Are you secure in your own beliefs and resilient in your response? As you 'come into your own' can you let go of the old way of thinking and have the courage of your own convictions? Using visualisation will assist you in staying focused and supporting yourself as you transform.

You may be met with criticism and judgement. Can you call on your wisdom, trust your higher power and have the courage to lead from the heart?

Once you have developed your personal formula by crystallising your goals according to your values, motivations and talents and aligning this to your higher purpose, then you have found gold. You can give yourself permission to follow through and trust. Develop a fail-safe plan so you can back yourself when doubt creeps in and can stay aligned to what is true and right for you. No longer do you need to look outside of yourself for permission to be and do what you would like; you can now do it all yourself. It's almost a relief as well as exciting to see what will come of it all.

Have you ever asked yourself who you are? Knowing who you are is necessary for defining your true comfort zone. It allows you to be authentic, to release yourself from all those aspects of your life that are not really you, that are just expectations of others. When I ask my clients who they are, most of them say, 'I don't know' or say something like, 'I'm a wife, a mother, a good cook and I work in a shop' or 'I'm a father and a husband and I work as a builder'.

'Ah ha, but who are you really?' I ask. 'What do you feel about …? What are you really thinking about? How has your life gone so far? Is it what you wanted in the first place? What are you here for?'

A common response from my clients has been, 'I just want my life back'.

'What stopped you doing something about it?' I ask.

The client takes a big breath and says something like, 'Oh well, I went to Uni, met my partner, we got married and before we knew it, we had two kids. But I never felt quite right about it. Just went along and did what was expected and what other folks were doing. I thought it was the right thing at the time. And don't get me wrong, my partner is a lovely person and I love my kids but I'm approaching forty now and I just feel unsettled. There's things I want to do and I'm afraid I'll never do them.'

'How long have you known this?'

'About nine years'

'How long have you been married?'

'About ten. We just live parallel lives. My partner looks after the kids and I go to work. We have friends over sometimes, but I know something is missing. I seem to have everything but I'm not happy. We don't talk like we used to, and I sometimes ask myself, is this all there is? I've done all the right things, what my parents advised, but something just doesn't feel right.'

'Anything else?' I ask.

'Hmm, yes. I'm feeling attracted to someone at work. She is alive and fun and looks after herself, you know, takes time to get dressed up. And she's always smiling and laughing. She's happy to see me and it makes me feel pretty damn good. And no, I haven't acted on it, but I've been very tempted to do so. It could be so easy. But no.'

I see my client looking wistfully away.

Then turning back to me, he assures me, or should I say, assures himself, and says, 'That's why I have come to see you, as I don't want to jeopardise my marriage. What can I do? I am so miserable. I'm between a rock and a hard place.'

'Have you told your partner what you think and feel at the moment?' I ask.

'She just half listens and says it will pass.'

I validate my client and acknowledge his loyalty and honesty, especially having the courage to come forward and admit that something is not working.

I have heard this story a few times now, where a couple reach a stalemate in their relationship. Things become boring, routine and predictable. The flame has become just a glimmer and one or both are restless and starting to question what it's all about.

This, believe it or not, is a gift. Yes, a gift, as there is an opportunity to revitalise not only the marriage but also themselves and consequently each other.

Often people do what they believe is the right thing in their lives, but they haven't really taken the time to check in to see if it's really the right thing for them.

When I asked how long he had felt this way, he said nine years. How often do we have a feeling that something isn't quite right but we get swept along? We ignore our intuition, that little voice that says, 'But didn't you want such and such?'

When I asked him to rewind to that time and think about what he would have liked, what he would have done, my client said that he would have liked to have travelled overseas when he was young, but instead he put it on hold and got married. He said he didn't really tell anyone because getting married was more in line with the values of his family.

I asked what happened to that dream and he said, 'I just thought maybe I'd go later, and I threw myself into work and making my wife and family happy.'

As I worked with this client, he realised that his frustration was that he may never travel and do something exciting with his life. He was becoming complacent and accepting of his lot. He was in his perceived comfort zone but recognised that something wasn't right and he wanted more.

The interesting thing about this scenario is that he could have had it all.

He was secure and his children were on their way to starting university. Rather than give up, rather than blame himself or his wife, he could open up to her about what would be fun, and what his dreams were.

You see, we do need to work and raise a family. Most of the time the marriage works well enough, often with the husband and wife both busy working, looking after the home and bringing up the children. But all too often a rift develops between them and it gradually gets wider. If you let it go too long the divide becomes too wide, it can become too hard to repair.

So, I worked with my client for a while – around twelve sessions over ten months. Once he realised he could actually have it all, that he could make some travel plans, take time off work and actually have a few more holidays, his energy started to lift. He also started playing golf on Saturdays to get out with his mates and reconnect with his business associates. He started to get excited.

Then he became quite anxious and was worried about what his wife would think about the change that he was going through, about asking for what he wanted and putting that to her.

As he was reconnecting to himself he realised he was fun-loving, sporty and adventurous. He needed to acknowledge this and validate himself enough to be able to express to his wife who he really was and to do this without threatening the relationship by having her feel insecure in any way.

He identified what his values were to see whether they were playing out in all areas of his life – work life, home life and socially. He worked out how he was driven and what his talents were. This gave him confidence as he started to build a truer self-identity. He listed the things that he would like to do in the next five years. They included taking his wife on a romantic cruise, travelling to Southeast Asia and having friends over after golf. He also realised that he had let his health and fitness go, so he worked on maintaining a really good level of fitness and with that became more confident.

The main hurdle for him was to ignore external expectations and give himself permission to not only have these things, but to let his wife know that this is what he needed now and involve her in the change.

And it was a huge change. He took little steps at first, and once he realised that he could do this, be more confident and be happier in defining himself and his needs, he realised the value of it and encouraged his wife to do the same.

He reported that she was a little hesitant and I offered that they both come in together to set goals both individually and as a couple. Through this it became clear that for the most part she felt the same. She wanted to go out with her girlfriends a bit more, she wanted more fun in her life and she definitely wanted to have a holiday. She felt that she had been just working for everyone else and, like her husband, had lost herself in raising a family. It was a relief and very exciting for them to see that they were actually wanting the same things. They had become too busy and had lost their way. They went off happily to plan and within a year they had reinvigorated their marriage, had fun and felt much more confident when it came to communicating to each other about what they wanted in the future.

The reason I'm telling you this is that we need time out of our lives to assess who we are and whether we are doing what we want – whether we are on track. It grieves me to see people on a treadmill and never taking charge of setting time aside to keep their lives alive and fulfilled when doing so can be so simple. This couple were comfortable, they were secure, and they were safe, they were in their perceived comfort zone, but life had become boring and restrictive. It took the guy to realise that there must be something more, it took him the courage to admit that he wasn't quite happy or fulfilled.

For my client to get to his true comfort zone, to do what he knew was right for him, meant going through some anxiety, going through change. He wanted to honour his marriage, and part of him knew that there was something more to be had. Together he and his wife developed their goals, including pursuing their hobbies, travelling and having fun socially. This was their true comfort zone where they felt fully alive and on track. It was easy, it was fun, and they felt connected and passionate with each other and in their marriage, and lots of wonderful opportunities started to come to them.

If society could realise and accept that it is better to acknowledge that things are not quite right – that we have down days, that we can go through difficult times in our relationships, that our businesses can have rough patches and that these are all normal occurrences, it would be much better. Once we realise this, we can get on with what we need to do to rectify the situation, and that can become more the norm than pretending that things are fine when they're not and burying our head in the sand.

We need time out of our lives to assess who we are and whether we are doing what we want – whether we are on track.

Creating yourself

Trust yourself. When we define ourselves by others, we run the risk of losing ourselves. When we define ourselves by our own sense of knowing, then we find ourselves. The essential requirement for spiritual growth on our personal development journey is trust.

I know when I went through hard times that I lost trust. I didn't believe there was a higher power or higher purpose for me. It wasn't until I had tried everything possible that I realised that trust was the only thing left that I hadn't tried or accepted. I now believe that my purpose was to acknowledge the good that already existed. It was all around me, but I couldn't see it. I was afraid to trust again.

Embrace who you are and with no emotion just step into it.

Step into your forté. Know that you are safe, as no

one can argue with this truth – that God-given gift that you have – and with all of your being, dare to be you.

There is something about you that is consistent, permanent and unchanging. It's almost as if when it comes to the crunch, this is who you are. People look at horoscopes and personality profiles to get some sense and meaning as to who they are, but there is a point where we know whether what they say sits with us or not.

So, who is that? Who is that person at your core who questions what is said by the horoscope? Who reads the personality profile and thinks, Yes, that's me, or No, they've got that wrong.

There is a fascination with knowing who we are, with finding ourselves, our identity, what drives us and what our purpose and meaning is in this world.

We all have a deep desire to know what our true essence is, where we have come from and our destiny. This is the question that most often comes up. And at the heart of it is a yearning to use our potential and have a more meaningful and fulfilled life.

It seems possible to develop clarity about our values, our beliefs, our motivations and aspirations, and to make some sense of it all, package it up and say this is who I am. But is it?

We are the culmination of experiences, the genes that

have been passed on to us – nurture and nature – and what we believe about ourselves, which is formulated in the first seven years of our lives. We go on, maintaining the scenario we have built for ourselves. It continuously repeats. It's what we consider or believe is our identity. We hold onto it with certainty, believing it is who we are, until one day we are challenged. This challenge could be in the form of losing something, not getting into a job or university, not getting a promotion, experiencing a relationship breakup or becoming ill. All of these things challenge the concept that we have of ourselves and give us the opportunity to reassess, renegotiate and re-evaluate who we think we are in this world.

Who is this constant who is doing the reassessing, the re-evaluating and the renegotiating? Who is creating the narrative, the story? We have our thoughts, our feelings, our memories and our dreams. What underpins that?

Generally we don't take time to think about this. We don't take time out of our lives and give ourselves a chance to connect to that piece of us that we come to understand is all-knowing and true. We get caught up in the busyness of life, making excuses that we don't have time, that we can't possibly take time out to assess who we are and what we want in our lives.

We each need to create an opportunity in some part of our lives where it can be free-flowing; those quiet moments when we challenge ourselves to think about whether we are on the right path or not for ourselves.

Paul Broks, a clinical neuropsychologist, says, 'We have a deep intuition that there is a core, an essence there and it's hard to shake off, probably impossible to shake off, I suspect. But it's true that neuroscience shows that there is no centre in the brain where things do all come together.'[16] Philosopher Julian Baggini agrees. There are lots of different processes in the brain, he explains, all of which operate, in a way, quite independently. And because of the way they relate we get this sense of self, a sense of comfort, by imagining that inside of us is something more unified than there really is.[17]

So, it's not about finding yourself, it's about creating yourself. You are not your past or your future. You are who you are right now, because in any given moment your energy can and will change. Letting go of the attachment saying, 'This is who I am' gives you the opportunity to allow so much more into your life. When we have a fixed view, then we stay stuck. If we think of ourselves as a moving, changing energy and spirit that is here to serve and transform, then we can keep discovering so much about ourselves – preferably for the good of others. I consider this liberating, expanding and very exciting.

Our ego can get caught up in the definition of who we are. For me, I have been a nurse, classical ballet dancer, artistic director of a classical ballet school, student of psychology, life coach, counsellor and executive performance coach – a lifelong learner.

But who am I in all that? What's the consistent, the commonality, the spirit, the energy that I bring? That, I believe, is who I am. Identify it; we all have it in us to search for our purpose and find meaning.

For me, when I step back to understand my true self as opposed to the selves that I've created to win approval and love, I realise it is quite different. Not only have I hidden myself from the world, I've hidden myself from myself because I was afraid of judgement, criticism and invalidation. The challenge for me to be myself was quite scary as I was often not allowed to express who I believed I was growing up. I wanted to win love and approval and it cost me greatly.

Writing this book has been an interesting exercise because what I have been offering and doing for my clients is certainly what I needed to offer and do for myself.

They say the thing you teach is what you most need

to learn, and for me this is very true. I was inspiring and motivating my clients to succeed. I was offering compassion and a safe place for them to be able to express their true desires. I was offering them a hand to hold metaphorically so as to empower them, to walk with them while they developed their strategies and actions to achieve what they wanted, to become who they believe they are. My life has been a continuum of trying to get into my true comfort zone – and here I am!

Writing this, I realised that I had taken bits and pieces of my own advice, but I had not fully gone through the process that I take my clients through. After all, how authentic am I if I haven't really used this method or concept myself to be and do the best that I can be? So, as I've been writing about the process for this book, I have also been taking myself through each step. The process has worked for my clients and they have achieved some fantastic results. But I realised that I needed to be a living example as well.

In order to take myself through the process, I needed to allow myself to be vulnerable, to be authentic, to show compassion to myself, to manage my energy and to be resilient. I needed to believe in myself and align myself to my higher purpose.

These are all the things I value in my own life and that I bring to the coaching process.

I also learnt humility. I am constantly humbled by what occurs in a coaching relationship, when I face a client and sit with them in deep respect, as they trust me with their vulnerabilities. I am honoured to have this gift. This gift is what I am, who I am. As one client said when I asked him why he chose me as a coach: 'I needed to know that I could trust a woman again.'

To now have the opportunity to share my experience is in itself another gift, and I am grateful to offer you my understanding of this realisation. It is just one way of viewing the world. I am certainly no academic; I have limited degrees but I have a lifetime of researching and, as one client said, a PhD in life experience.

So when you consider who you are it's not about the house you live in, the car you drive, the school your children are at. It's not about your relationship, being beautiful, or about prestige. When you take all this away what are you left with? What's your character? What are the qualities standing in front of you? What can you work with now? When you stand naked and open and vulnerable, who are you then?

In my experience working as an intern at a rehabilitation hospital, I witnessed clients being vulnerable. Some say that vulnerability is weakness; however, what I saw was an unwavering inner strength and willingness to be there for themselves. I ask you, could you do this? Could you stand there open and vulnerable whilst backing yourself at the same time?

This to me is true strength. I have been in this place. When you have the no-care factor, meaning when you have nothing else to lose, you have to develop an 'I don't care' attitude. There is nothing else, so what more do you have to do? I surrendered. It's a place where I felt relief. Life was simple and I was open to what opportunities could arise. It was all down to me. It was then that I asked myself: Who am I? I continue to ask myself even now. And now I ask you: Who are you in all of this?

From the time we are born, we are given a name and told all kinds of things about ourselves. These details, opinions and ideas become facts that go towards building ourselves, our identity. And that self becomes the vehicle for navigating our social world. But that self is an image based on other people's projections. Hence the question: Is this who we really are?

When I was dancing I would literally lose myself. I could put all my emotional expression into my dancing. I could feel the energy surging through my body – in my limbs, my fingertips and toes, in the strength of my legs, in the grace of my hands. It was a vehicle for me to express my real self. It allowed a safe space that I could visit, where I could express all of the emotions in a non-destructive way. I felt grounded and suspended by my essence. I felt completely connected. I was myself. I learned how to trust my higher self.

As a student of classical ballet, I learnt to work towards a peak performance level where I couldn't make mistakes or falter as the dance would ultimately be affected. I couldn't risk being off-balance while pirouetting on my point shoe, as I would fall over.

I was trained by a Russian teacher who taught me that 'There is no such thing as can't.' She taught me the meaning of excellence, consistency, perseverance, determination and most of all the love of ballet.

When I was the artistic director of a ballet school, I had trained one of my students to major level. She was about to go into her exam when she froze at the entrance to the room. Looking at me desperately she said, 'Miss Sue, I can't remember my dance.'

This student was highly trained, had practised until it was automatic and knew her dance intimately, but in that moment she had allowed the anxiety of wanting to do well and meet her own high expectations to overcome her thinking. She had gone into doubt about her ability to perform her dance.

Her level of anxiety had risen so high that it had moved past the tipping point of optimal anxiety and had increased to a level where she was entering the danger zone and wouldn't be able to complete her dance effectively.

I took her by the hand, looked her in the eye and asked, 'What are you here for? What are you really here for?'

She took a deep breath and with gusto said, 'I just want to dance. I just want to dance.' With that her shoulders relaxed. It was like a wave of relief had washed over her at the realisation that she could do what she loved. She entered the room and danced to her heart's delight. She had got in touch with what she loved, what her passion was and what her end game was, which was to be a dancer. Her doubts dissipated and her reason became crystal clear.

How many times do we fill our minds with the clutter of doubt and miss out on opportunities to excel?

How can we capture that ability to trust the spiritual component in our performance?

Many studies have been done on peak performance in athletes, but now they are researching ballet dancers as they are regarded not only as elite athletes but as performing artists as well.

Lynda Flower conducted a study of the spiritual aspect of peak performance in classical ballet performers.[18] She found that for many former dancers, 'in the zone' experiences in their performance and subsequent teaching had changed their world view and had a positive lasting influence. For some dancers, she explained, these experiences 'generated an ongoing sense of achievement and "making a difference", while for others, the "in the zone" feelings of joy, freedom and abandonment increased intuitive awareness and the ability to handle stress more effectively'.

I have experienced this transcendent state in dance, and I have called on it in my life when needed, and I still do. First as a dance teacher and now as a performance coach and writer.

Flow

If you want to increase your wellbeing, creativity, and productivity then you might want to cultivate *flow*, a concept describing those moments when you're completely absorbed in a challenging but doable task.

The Hungarian-American psychologist Mihaly Csikszentmihalyi developed the concept of flow. In his book *Flow: The psychology of optimal experience* he writes that flow is 'the state in which people are so involved in an activity that nothing else seems to matter; the experience itself is so enjoyable that people will do it even at a great cost, for the sheer sake of doing it.'[19]

In my experience of dancing and teaching classical ballet, the aim in executing a dance move was that it must be practised over and over until it became automatic and second nature and with little chance of making mistakes. The technique had to be perfected so that you could do it without consciously thinking about it. When you felt this confident then the option of external influences, thoughts, opinions or emotional arousal would not sway your ability to execute the 'enchainment' or dance.

Working hard on the technique, practising until you can't get it wrong, meant that you could enter the zone where you don't have to consciously think. You would be able to then focus your attention on musicality, the audience and the character of the dancer.

I believe that once I mastered the physical performance level required, then I found myself entering the 'flow state' where it then became easy. I was able to use that level and then, for instance, choreograph a ballet at that level. When choreographing a ballet, I would have an idea or hear the music, see the dance movements in my mind and then it just flowed. Time would pass and before I knew it hours had gone by. In my experience, I had transcended into a state where nothing else mattered, I was totally absorbed in creativity.

In dance, this achievement of your own personal excellence – your optimal performance zone – is a balance of your skills and your interest or challenge level in the performance.

If you become overly anxious, as my student did, instead of staying at your optimal performance zone you would find yourself at the tipping point and enter the panic or danger zone. The aim here is to understand your level of abilities and work hard to increase this performance level without pushing too hard, creating to much anxiety and compromising your achievement.

When you become more competent and couple that with a realistic view of your performance level, then your confidence increases and you have a better chance at not only performing the task or exercise but being able to build on it to increase your capacity.

It takes strength of mind to consistently improve and perfect your technique. When performing a dance, it is both demanding and challenging, as you need to have practised each step to execute it individually with perfect technique and then seamlessly put each step together. Not only is it done in a sequence, but it must be musically in time, demonstrate the dynamics of the dance and express the artistry required to make it look effortless to the audience. This takes years of practise and commitment coupled with physical agility, coordination and timing.

A dancer learns to overcome distractions and to keep going. Hence the term 'the show must go on'. Having that level of internal fortitude and confidence means that you can recover quickly, regain composure and move forward with your dance. And, dare I say, this applies in your performance in any area in your life.

When an individual is in the flow state there is a loss of the awareness of time. I know that when writing this book, I experienced flow. My level of interest and challenge and my skills of writing were equally matched. If, however, I became frustrated by the techniques of writing the book, then the motivation dropped. Once I realised that asking for help from my editor was needed, then my motivation increased.

I was intrinsically motivated as I am intensely curious and passionate about this whole topic. Time would pass and I realised that I hadn't eaten; I was totally comfortable and enjoying the flow state. I was absorbed fully in my internal thinking processes and, dare I say, became mildly irritated if someone or something interrupted my thinking whilst I was in that zone.

In both the optimal performance zone and the flow state, anxiety can be an interference to maintaining the level of concentration required.

When I asked my student 'What are you really here for?' and she said, 'I just want to dance', she tapped into a crucial element, and that was that she loved to dance. When I asked my client what he loved about landing the deal, suddenly everything became clear for him. The anxiety levels dissipated in both instances. They galvanised their thinking and their mission became crystal clear.

I'll put the question to you again: Are you afraid to get out of your perceived comfort zone or are you really afraid to get into your true comfort zone?

In my view, I believe it requires a unique level of trust, a trust in yourself, a trust in your love of what you do, and a trust in your higher power, whatever that is for you.

In order to experience freedom and fulfillment you need to learn how to minimise internal and external interferences while you continually build your self-confidence, stay aligned to your motivations and, most of all, recognise your passion and love of the activity.

Self-transcendence

American psychologist Abraham Maslow developed a motivation theory based on a hierarchy of needs. He defines transcendence as 'the very highest and most inclusive or holistic levels of human consciousness, behaving and relating, as ends rather than means, to oneself, to significant others, to human beings in general, to other species, to nature, and to the cosmos'.[20]

I agree with Maslow's model when he states that at the level of self-actualisation, the individual works to actualise their own potential using their creativity, talents and abilities. At the level of transcendence, the individual's own needs are second to their service to others. I believe that this is when you can let go of ego and operate from a higher purpose.

Peak experiences are important to achieving a transcendent state. These are moments of pure joy and elation and bring a sense of abandonment. Individuals often liken them to a spiritual experience. This is evident in classical ballet dancers.

Peak experiences occur when you maximise your talents and your potential.

Viktor Frankl, an Austrian neurologist, psychiatrist and holocaust survivor, explained how he suffered terribly during WWII but was able to tap into thinking that we ultimately have a choice.

My favourite quote from his book, *Man's Search for Meaning*, is 'Everything can be taken from a man but one thing: the last of the human freedoms – to choose one's attitude in any given set of circumstances, to choose one's own way'.

When you lose everything suddenly all that's around you becomes clear. You realise what really matters in life so that you can survive. I believe that once you realise this then you can let go of your own needs and be of service to others. This is when you operate from your higher purpose.

As Frankl said in his book, 'we who lived in concentration camps can remember the men who walked through the huts comforting others, giving away their last piece of bread'.

The more you align yourself to your true nature and trust your higher power, the more you will have the courage to trust and be open to your true comfort zone.

CHAPTER 9

Your true comfort zone

Your true comfort zone is where you lead from your heart, align to your higher purpose and live with a sense of freedom and fulfillment. It is your innate talent – your natural genius. Connect with what it is that you bring to the world, connect with why you really do what you do, then connect with what you are really here for.

When you take off the layers that you have accepted in life to be where you are now, you have the choice to feel the freedom of being you, and to build on that based on the essence of who you are. It's a wonderful and enlightening process to eventually find yourself and then build your life based on your definition of you.

To find your true comfort zone, I've developed a

package – a culmination of all of the activities I have suggested in the book, based on my education and life experience. I have gone through this process myself and encouraged my clients to as well. When you take the time, the energy and the money to invest in you, I believe you give yourself the greatest gift of all.

Finding your true comfort zone means becoming clear about what your fort is that you have created and presented to the world and being brave enough to challenge the status quo. It's about being honest and having the courage to take a stand and redefine your personal vision; getting really clear about your values, motivations and talents; getting confident about the beliefs that will support you, moving forward; tapping into your sense of knowing – what is true and right for you in any given circumstance; accepting that this is who you are and trusting yourself in each moment; developing strategies to support yourself when you are being tested; knowing that you can come back to your personal formula or package; and knowing each moment who you are being in all of this. When you know all of this, you will develop the strength to quietly and confidently withstand whatever life throws at you.

As you stand at the edge of your future, know that

you have a choice. You can choose to stay safe in your fort with the familiar and be content with that. Or, if you are restless, you can choose to take a step on the journey to freedom and fulfillment – choose energy, excitement, health, opportunities, self-esteem, confidence, personal achievement and peak performance and trust.

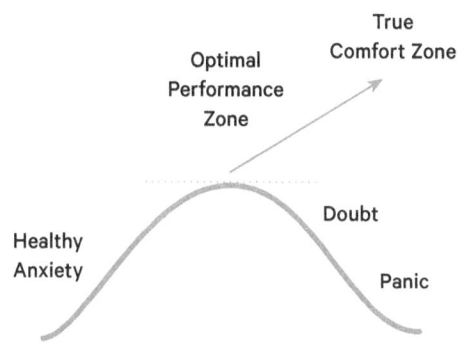

WHAT ARE YOU HERE FOR?

Why is the true comfort zone good for you? Because it creates meaning in your life, fulfilment, the freedom to be who you truly are. Your health and wellbeing increase so that you are full to overflowing – so much so that you have a reserve and can give back without feeling depleted. You feel relief to not only know who you are, but to be that person fully and calmly.

So, ask yourself: What are you passionate about? What do you love?

This journey to your true comfort zone is about addressing how you present currently in your perceived comfort zone. Is it really you? Peel a layer away and you'll find that you have some fears and doubts that you may need to address and reframe your thinking about. Then peel the next layer away and you become really clear about your talents, motivations and values – who you really are. Then you'll have your package, your formula, ready. It will endure because it is who you are, and no one can argue with that.

Then you commit to transforming into what you know to be true and right for you. You then give yourself permission to be that person in whatever capacity that might be. I'm not saying that you will always be performing well or be in a constant flow state. You will experience being vulnerable, you'll be scared at times, and you will also be excited and exceptional.

There is, however, that one thing that is a constant – your true comfort zone. When you develop your true comfort zone formula, it will endure, because it is truly who you are. When you choose your true comfort zone, you create the opportunity to stand in your own power with ease and grace, aligned with your higher power and trusting your higher purpose. You will experience greater joy and peace of mind.

Armed with your fail-safe formula, do you have the courage of your own convictions?

I have found that even though I experienced all the assessments, therapy and profiling tools, there was still something else at work.

When you are completing the exercises in this book, you may find that you question them; maybe they don't all feel right for you to complete one. Perhaps it's not the right time for you. You see, most people think that a profiling tool or personal development exercise is the answer, but as you do the exercises you will find that you are assessing the assessment. Who is the one who really knows? Listen to the whisper. Some call it intuition or a gut feeling. You also need to factor in your life experience when making your decisions.

Understanding your values will help clarify who you are. Then you can step into your true comfort zone and achieve what you never thought possible. Values are a crucial part of your life. They account for more than ninety percent of your everyday decisions. They drive your behaviours and, I believe, underpin everything that you do and believe about yourself. To reach your true comfort zone you need to identify your values and ensure they are aligned with what you want to be and do in your life.

When I take my clients through the values exercise I ask them to choose approximately twenty-five values that they believe are important to them. I then ask them to choose from that list, the five values most important to them. These are their core values. After that we explore different areas of their life such as health and wellbeing, career, home environment, finances, relationships and business to see how these values are playing out, or are not playing out in those areas. This then gives them an awareness of how aligned they are to those values. If any areas of their life aren't aligned with their values, then we develop strategies to have them more in sync.

Defining your values helps you to understand what you stand for and, more importantly, what you don't stand for. Since they underpin everything that we do, if our actions are not aligned with all of our core values it may cause grief in one or more facets of our lives.

I believe our purpose in life is closely interwoven with our values. They are a core part of our personality and play a role in unifying our behaviours. Our values influence the way we respond to people and events; they direct and motivate us towards certain goals; and influence our choice of career and partners.

In my opinion, if you look at Richard Branson it seems evident that one of his values is fun. He has the ability to attract people because of his fun-loving nature, and this has helped to open up business opportunities for him.

My values are competence, time freedom, quality of life, elegance (the quality of being pleasingly ingenious and simple[21]) and financial security. But there is one value above all of those: family. When I am on track in my life and my business and being aligned to my values, family will override all the other values, so I will jump and deal with people in my family over everything else. Being conscious of this is helpful for me in terms of being able to set a boundary and develop a strategy so that I stay aligned to what is ultimately for my highest good.

When we discover and clarify our personal values, it is important that these are in harmony with those in our workplace. Most people naturally want to make a difference in their work environment and by attaining a good match between personal values and those of the organisation, peak performance can be enhanced. When you have your own business, your personal values are likely to be similar to your business values.

My business values for Invest in You® are compassion, authenticity, resilience and energy management. When

I look at these it is interesting to note how they fit with my personal values. Am I aligned to these values? The answer is 'yes'.

When you work in a large organisation, however, these values may be different. Quite often people work for an organisation or business that their personal values are not aligned to, and this can be quite challenging. Their values may be constantly at odds with the behaviours that occur at work and what they are expected to do in their job. Ideally, if your values align with the organisation you work for, then you are more likely to be fulfilled in your role.

Simply being conscious and aware of your values assists you in defining who you are in each moment. That's why I think it is imperative to take time out to invest in you and to assess what your values really are, so in each moment you can handle anything that occurs in your life based on what is true for you.

You feel fulfilled when you live according to your values in each area of your life. You get a sense of satisfaction and achievement because you are not compromising yourself. You are honouring what is truly meaningful for you. Hence, not compromising your integrity. It makes life somewhat easier to navigate. Our values also determine what we will move towards or away from in terms of our life purpose and goals. When you can identify your values and live by them, it moves you towards ultimately attaining your true comfort zone.

Once my clients are aware of their values I ask them to name five values that are important to them that they would like to move towards. They may wish to achieve greater security in their life, for example, or have more freedom.

I then ask them to identify feeling states they need in order to create these values in their lives. Common responses are self-belief, focus and determination .

You feel fulfilled when you live according to your values in each area of your life.

Goals

Once my clients have established their values I support them to clarify their goals and to align their energy and intentions toward success.

Getting clear on your purpose comes down to an awareness of what helps you feel in alignment. Knowing your values can help you keep on track, validate yourself, and honour and follow your direction.

If you start working towards a goal but it feels a little

rigid and forced, or you are uncomfortable in any way, or are trying too hard to make it happen, then it could be time to correct your course. Let go of your need to control the outcome and tune in to what you could work towards that would allow you to feel more aligned and more in flow, more in the zone. When we do get clear on our goals and our bigger vision and purpose, it may mean that we need to let go of old goals and give ourselves permission to change our mind even though at times this may feel quite disconcerting.

I firmly believe that being in alignment with your true comfort zone is about living in a way that serves and supports your highest good, that honours your values and passions, and that guides you to listen to your intuition, your inner wisdom and guidance, your infinite self.

Mind you, when you are in alignment it isn't necessarily a guarantee that you'll experience smooth sailing all the time. But when you have a challenge you will have the inner strength and resilience to survive and thrive, and to come out more devoted to yourself. You will know that you have the ability to handle it.

In challenging times it's important to be mindful of your energy and to recalibrate when necessary. This could be in the form of a yoga class, bush walk or time out sitting on a park bench. Spend some time reassessing and thinking about whether you are on the right track and still aligned with your values. This develops a deeper sense of trust in yourself and with the universe. Simply release yourself from your expectations, integrate the lessons learnt, recalibrate and top up your energy. Set new goals and get clear on your dreams to help you find your flow again.

Trust yourself. Accept yourself. Acknowledge your failures and the lessons they contain. Recognise that in every moment you are doing the best that you can given what you have and what you know at the time.

CASE STUDY

Do you remember Norman back in Chapter 2? Two years after he completed his sessions with me, I rang him to have a follow-up talk and see how he was going. He shared with me that he had since landed two more developments. I was so pleased for him. We got talking and he said he was happy for me interview him for this book. He felt honoured to be asked and I was excited to explore further how the true comfort zone had worked for him.

Norman's father travelled a lot with his job in the military and Norman learnt French until he was eight years old. He was then moved to an English-speaking school. At this very early age he had to leave his home – all that was familiar to him. Norman found spelling English difficult at times, and consequently reading and writing were challenging for him. This big jump out of his perceived comfort zone had left him assuming that he was dyslexic.

I asked Norman what it has been like getting out of his perceived comfort zone since we finished our sessions.

'I believe that what's big really isn't. Just have a crack at it and see what happens.'

I also asked him if his perceived comfort zone is really comfortable.

'Building the childcare centres is great. I get to use all of my skills and experience, and now I can just keep doing it each time. I've developed the formula and it works. It is a great success.'

'So, are you in your true comfort zone now?'

'Yes, but there was something that I still wanted to do to "right the wrong".'

The thread running through Norman's life to this point was this desire to 'right the wrongs'.

'At fourteen years I was running a little wild. Then my father passed away. With his passing, I realised that I wanted to live my life and do it my way.'

Norman had wanted to join the Air Force Cadets when he was fourteen years old, so he could train to eventually become a pilot. He was not allowed to go forward because of his eyesight, though. Instead, he joined the police force where he worked until he realised that his values weren't aligned with the organisation and it was very hard to 'right the wrongs'. He said the experience was akin to the song 'It's a Mad World'.

Norman moved to Australia and was to participate in the 1984 Olympics as a member of the fencing team, but at the last minute he decided it wasn't for him.

He then became involved in property development, building childcare centres. He realised the value of making sure that the first seven years of a child's life were safe, creative and productive. This would give them a good start in life.

Once he had developed a substantial property portfolio, he decided to take some trial lessons flying a helicopter.

'I have built all of the centres and now I am in a position to learn how to fly helicopters. I went to an airport and thought that I would do some trial lessons. My eyesight is limited for long and short distance and I decided to have a laser operation to correct it. I am giving myself permission to do it now. That means that I can finally fly. Now I can do it!'

Norman was finally fulfilling his potential and coming into his own. This was his true comfort zone – what he knew was right for him.

'What is it like to be in your true comfort zone now?'

'When I'm in my true comfort zone I feel proud and honourable. It gives me a sense of purpose. When I am flying it feels like a holiday – I was addicted from the first hour. I'm in the bubble and in the zone. My true comfort zone.'

Norman's perceived comfort zone involved staying safe from feeling the disapproval of his family. He was holding himself back from growing his business and realising his true potential. When he had the courage to look at his situation, he could release his doubts, overcome his fears and identify who he really was. He was then able to give himself permission to do what he knew to be true and right for him, to back himself and come into his own – to step into his true comfort zone.

Norman's journey is a great example of doing what we think we should and finding that it isn't quite right for us. He felt unsettled but was able to tease out what it really was that meant so much for him.

Norman did a full circle and was able to fly, which was what he wanted in the first place. He had the courage to honour his heart's desire.

Motivation

Desire is the key to motivation, but it's a determined commitment to an unrelenting pursuit of your goal, a commitment to excellence, that will enable you to attain the success you seek.

Motivation is the driving force that makes you feel

glad to be jumping out of bed in the morning, excited and looking forward to your day. When you have it, it is energising, exciting, enlivening. Don't make the mistake of thinking that the dynamic and motivated people you know are lucky to be that way. Getting motivated and staying motivated is an art form that we actually need to learn.

Motivated people are passionate. They don't need to be loud, they can present with just an intense, quiet confidence. They love what they do. Their enthusiasm and excitement is infectious and this attracts other people's interest.

When we have a goal in mind, we might sometimes start it but then not follow through. We can get sidetracked or disappointed by an early setback. We are on a high, experiencing that first flush of excitement at the prospect of achieving this new goal, only to find that the energy and commitment seem to run out all too soon.

There are many reasons we become demotivated. Sometimes I feel that I haven't followed through on something because my dream was unrealistic, but then I realise I didn't create a workable action plan. Sometimes it can be that the goal isn't really right for us. Sometimes we let our beliefs get in the way: we doubt ourselves, the greatest dampener of enthusiasm. Sometimes we don't initiate a good strategy and a plan to follow with some effective actions that keep us on track and motivated. Sometimes we don't put an accountability buddy or a good coach into the equation to make sure that we stay on track. The important thing is to focus on your vision. Stay focused on your vision because it will inspire you to maintain persistence and determination so that you will never give up.

To achieve your goals, you must have passion, you must really believe in what you are doing. You must be persistent and determined to do what you want. You must stay on purpose and implement your plans and strategies. The most important aspect to achieving your goals, though, is that you must have some reason that surpasses all else. A reason that underpins all that you do and gives meaning to the everyday actions that you must do each day to succeed. A reason that is aligned with your values, your true self.

My goal was to write this book. It's not easy to write a book. I had to write down my processes and experiences, evaluate the techniques that I use, and work out anecdotally what was successful and what was not so successful. I worked on it for six hours each day, which I tell you was not easy for me. So you may ask, why did I do it?

Because I want to give hope, I want to spread my message that you can be, do and have all that you desire if you have the courage to step into your true comfort zone.

As I sit here reflecting on these processes, I too am learning about my journey – through the experiences of my clients and the experiences of my life. I am reaching the point where I finally arrive on stage to speak. I believe my message is important as we waste so much time in fear, doubt and insecurity. When we reach a high point in our life there can still be something missing. That is to trust in your higher purpose. When you trust in your higher purpose that is when you are in your true comfort zone.

When I was fourteen years old, I was at an awards night for school. It was the end of year awards night and my parents had come and were sitting up the back. We were in a huge auditorium and I was sitting there hoping that I would win an award, as you do when you're young. I had worked hard and thought perhaps I might receive a most-improved award. They went through all the awards and as the principal came near the end of them it was looking unlikely that I would receive anything. I got a bit distracted and my heart was sinking thinking, Oh well, not this year. All of a sudden over the loudspeaker I heard my name. I jumped with glee inside thinking that I would be recognised for some academic achievement; I had worked very hard to get my grades that year.

The award was announced. It was for being the kindest person in the school. I was so embarrassed. At fourteen years old my life was all about image and fitting in the cool group. I wanted to shrink under my chair and disappear, but no, I had to take a deep breath and walk down the very long aisle and up to the podium to receive my award, which was a set of praying hands. I walked – almost ran – back to my seat. Some of my friends came up to praise me, some of them laughed and some of them were looking at me quizzically – I'm still not sure what that was about. At some level I must have shown compassion and kindness and the school acknowledged that with the award. At that age I was embarrassed. I now see the wisdom in the school giving me the prize. It still brings a tear to my eye of sheer embarrassment as I recall that time, but now I recognise that the nuns could see the kindness and generosity of spirit in me and wanted to acknowledge it with an award.

Was I in my true comfort zone when I was being kind to others? I felt fulfilled, complete when others opened up to me. I was often a confidante to the other girls. It didn't drain me and I felt aligned to my higher purpose.

So, yes, I believe I was in my true comfort zone. I was in the flow, it was easy, and I absolutely loved it. And even though at that stage I absolutely loved being there for my friends.

Purpose

Imagine that you have to achieve some of your goals. Then ask yourself what these accomplishments give you. Your answers may reveal your values – what really drives you. You see, even though I had worked hard to achieve good results at school, I was still there for my friends – to listen and care for them. Even at that age I was looking for ways to help others and to contribute to their lives, although I didn't realise at the time that this was going to be a thread running throughout my life. My natural spirit was surpassing all else, and there is no way you can actually control that.

Your values demonstrate the essence of what really inspires you to reach for your dreams. Have a look at your list of goals and make a note of why you want to achieve them. It will help you to get to the core of what it is that really drives you.

Whenever you are working towards one of your key values, you will be highly motivated to succeed. Mother Teresa, Mahatma Gandhi and Nelson Mandela worked tirelessly helping others. Their dedication gave them power and resilience. It was their spirit. I believe they were in their true comfort zone. What they did was aligned with their higher power and in service to others.

Your values don't have to be earth-shattering and impressive in order for them to work for you. Think of the parent who gets up first thing in the morning, makes breakfast, prepares lunches, and smiles as they get the children off to school, even though they may have been up through the night with a crying toddler. It could be that they are aligned to their value of family and it all feels worthwhile.

Or think of the person who works tirelessly, day in and day out to provide for their family, even when they feel that they need a holiday; it could be that their value is pride or protection.

Take time to discover the deeper meaning and purpose behind your desire. Take time to know your values and your true purpose. When you connect to yourself in this way, you can then make a conscious decision to make your goals happen.

You are the only one who can make it happen for you. Others can offer a hand and support and encourage you, but you must find the energy and determination in order to step into the centre of your own life. To step into what I call your true comfort zone and take charge.

Any negative self-talk will demotivate you. You must be conscious about retraining your brain, your thought processes, to support you. This way you'll become more focused, effective and efficient.

Starting your day with a positive activity, such as going for a walk, listening to music or a podcast, or reading an inspiring chapter, will help set you up. Give yourself every opportunity to succeed.

Don't turn on the television or listen to the news until you have planned your day, and definitely do not open your inbox until you have your plan in place. Set your intention about how you want your day to play out, then you'll know what you need to do and be able to handle anything that comes up.

Talents

I use a profiling tool with my clients that helps them to identify their talents so they can operate at their best. A talent is a natural ability or aptitude: a special ability that allows someone to do something particularly well without being taught. It is quite often considered God-given. When have you felt embarrassed for standing out, for being different, for speaking up, for doing the right thing, for having people ask you for advice? Chances are you were displaying some talent or gift that should be nurtured and developed.

When I had my profile created with this tool, I found out what I kind of knew about myself, but didn't have the words for. Seeing the profile written down, though, gave me the confidence to go forward more resolutely and confidently. It confirmed that I was off track in a job that didn't work for my highest good. It also confirmed that I was too afraid to be the talented person I was meant to be.

Ironically, when I look back on my dancing career, I was using my talents when running my ballet school and I was quite naturally being very successful as a result of this. I ran the school with no analysing, no business skills, just by following my instincts and common sense.

It is important to understand your talents so you don't waste time and energy doing things that are not aligned with your natural ability, your innate talent. I had deviated from my natural talents and the profiling tool helped me reconnect with the track that was right and true for me.

Your true comfort zone

I have written this book to show you how to get into your true comfort zone. It is what I was meant to do. It is my unique talent, my gift. When you step into your true comfort zone you know that it is right for you – you are complete. It is unique to you – the zone where you feel fulfilled and free, where your natural genius is expressed and released. The relief surpasses all of your struggles; it is for your highest good.

Originally, I was helping clients to get out of their perceived comfort zone – to address the fears and doubts and insecurities that present as we endeavour to be more of who we are. The clients would identify where they wanted to be – a big leap for some – accept where they currently were in the scheme of things, then look at how they would take the steps to get there. But fears, doubts and insecurities were often present and disabled their thinking and impeded their progress.

As a coach, I could see their potential and visualise them attaining the outcome they wanted, but they couldn't see it. As an onlooker, I would imagine it to be so easy for them, but how could I assist them through the pain and challenges at a faster rate? How could I make the journey gentler, smoother, easier, so that they would last to the end and the result would be the best for them and all concerned? How could I elevate them to a higher level so that they would fulfil their desires and ambitions and be true to their innate purpose?

During my own journey, I have explored dance, academia, counselling, hypnotherapy, psychology, massage and reiki, all to evolve and reach my potential – to tap into something that I knew existed, but could not put my finger on. It was about the connection to and trust of my true comfort zone. That it is okay. That I can rely on myself. That I will be enough to succeed. Giving myself permission to trust in myself again. I lost trust at five years of age when to survive, I had to be someone else. So I became a shell. I couldn't trust myself to be myself any more. I became the good girl. I retreated within my own shell and observed life through a glass cage. I was removed from the essence of who I am.

Since then I have learnt to trust myself, to step into my true comfort zone. And you can too.

CHAPTER 10

Standing at the edge of your future

I have explored the optimal performance zone, the flow state and Maslow's self-actualisation and self-transcendence.

In all of these states I have noticed that there is a desire to fulfill one's potential in some capacity. The people who first identified these states believed that there is something more at stake, to tap into a peak performance state, be it physical – mental or spiritual. There are many tools and avenues to self-discovery, but at the end of the day who is the voice that says, 'No, that's not for me', 'No, that's not the best for me', 'Yes, I agree with this' or 'This fits but that doesn't'? Who is that voice that whispers to you?

It's you. Only you know what is best for you.

A place of freedom and fulfilment

My definition of true comfort zone is that it is where you honour your natural talents, the full expression of who you are, aligned to your higher purpose – that place of freedom and fulfilment. And how do we arrive there? Through self-exploration, by tapping into the innate sense of knowing what is true and right for us.

As a child we are born open, trusting, loving, in awe of the world, full of potential and like a sponge, ready to soak up experiences. We take in the world around us. All of the views, experiences, self-esteem, self-worth and judgements are layered upon us. We absorb our carers' opinions and world views into our own being, and we define ourselves by those views and experiences. We adapt and are moulded to fit the world we grew up in so that we can survive.

And survive we do until we come to see that this world view, our perceived comfort zone, is not comfortable at all. At this stage, we have created a life that is supposed to be happy, but gradually the cracks appear and the questions and doubts surface.

This perceived comfort zone has served to get us so far, but now it's time to disrupt the status quo, pull aside the layers, reveal the illusion, question the beliefs, become uncomfortable and then decide differently.

It is our responsibility to ourselves to unravel the confusion, peel off the layers that don't serve us, that are not aligned to our values or our potential, and become crystal clear about who we are, accept now that this is who we were meant to be. And as we do that, we need to offer ourselves compassion and love. Then we can make new choices more aligned with our talents, values and motivations.

What does your original face look like? Give yourself permission as you tap into the wonder of you and to trust that it is okay to be that person. We spend our lives becoming someone, and now it's about unbecoming so that you can reveal the person you were meant to be. Rebuild your life according to what you know is true and right for you, according to your higher purpose.

Come home to your true comfort zone.

Your future

You have the option as you stand at the edge of your future, to stay in your perceived comfort zone or to step into your true comfort zone.

Your true comfort zone does not change. It is the true essence of who you are. It is your potential. When you go through this process of change, you will develop your true comfort zone formula, and, just like a lighthouse weathering the storm, you will hold steadfast to your higher purpose and know that it will surpass all else.

My question to you is: *Are you afraid of stepping out of your perceived comfort zone or are you really afraid of stepping into what you know is true and right for you, your true comfort zone?* Simply give yourself permission. It's a matter of allowing yourself the opportunity and believing enough to make it happen.

I could have shied away from writing this book and said, 'I'm not ready yet', but I thought that I would just give it a damn good go. What is one thing that you would like do that you have shied away from, that's keeping you in your perceived comfort zone?

Take a step towards what you know is true and right for you in your life. Use your creativity to create what you want, call on your years of wisdom so you can find meaning in your life. Only you know what is right for you.

When you are in your true comfort zone you derive pleasure from what you do and feel fully engaged in; what life has to offer for you. Your work performance increases, your wellbeing improves, and your relationships are enhanced. Stop being harsh on yourself, fill yourself with compassion and encouragement and simply take the step.

Like me, my clients are willing to admit when things aren't working so well. Together we sort out a strategy to move forward, so that they can become much more fulfilled, happier, live a life in line with their values, a life where they can get into their true comfort zone.

My business is about investing in you. What that means is taking the time to invest in yourself, making the effort to invest in yourself and investing money in yourself, because when you invest in you and keep developing personally, you will eventually reach your true comfort zone. Acknowledge your talents and gifts, trust yourself, connect with what is greater than you. Step into your true comfort zone, where you tap into your natural genius and do what is true and right for you.

Whatever you do or dream you can, begin it; Boldness has genius, magic and power in it. Begin it now.

Goethe

I believe that what most of us truly desire is to get into our true comfort zone – that place where you honour your natural talents, the full expression of who you are, which is aligned to your higher purpose.

Endnotes

1 White, A., 2008, 'From comfort zone to performance management: understanding development and performance', <www.academia.edu/460313/From_Comfort_Zone_to_Performance_Management>

2 Yerkes, R.M. & Dodson, J.D., 1908, 'The relation of strength of stimulus to rapidity of habit-formation', *Journal of comparative neurology and psychology*, 18, pp.459–482, <www.psychclassics.yorku.ca/Yerkes/Law/>

3 Walsch, N. D., 1995, *Conversations with God: An uncommon dialogue. Book 1*. New York: G. P. Putnam's Sons

4 Tracy, B. (n.d.). BrainyQuote.com. Retrieved 9 September 2019, from BrainyQuote.com, <www.brainyquote.com/quotes/brian_tracy_391332>

5 Brown, B. in Tugend, A., 2011, 'Tiptoeing out of one's comfort zone (and of course, back in)', *The New York Times*, 11 February, <www.nytimes.com/2011/02/12/your-money/12shortcuts.html>

6 Raghunathan, R., 2012, 'Familiarity breeds enjoyment', *Psychology Today*, 17 January, <www.psychologytoday.com/au/blog/sapient-nature/201201/familiarity-breeds-enjoyment>

7 Whitmore, J., 2017, *Coaching for performance*, 5th edition. London: John Murray Press

8 Hamilton, D. R., 2011, 'Visualisation alters the brain & body', Using science to inspire, April 19, David R Hamilton PhD, <www.drdavidhamilton.com/visualisation-alters-the-brain-body/>

9   www.theneuroacademy.com/

10 Fox, E. (n.d.). Goodreads.com. Retrieved 9 September 2019, from Goodreads.com. <https://www.goodreads.com/quotes/231964-do-it-trembling-if-you-must-but-do-it>

11 Dobson, A., 'What is procrastination', *Mindfit Hypnosis*, < www.mindfithypnosis.com/what-is-procrastination/>

12 Robbins, M., 2018, 'The 5 second rule', *Mel Robbins*, 1 May, <www.melrobbins.com/blog/the-5-second-rule/>

13 Sinek, S., 'Find your WHY', Simon Sinek < www.simonsinek.com/find-your-why/>

14 Thoreau, H. D. (n.d.), BrainyQuote.com. Retrieved 10 September 2019, from BrainyQuote.com, < www.brainyquote.com/quotes/henry_david_thoreau_163655>

15 Caprino, K., 2014, '6 Ways pushing past your comfort zone is critical to success', *Forbes*, 21 May, <www.forbes.com/sites/kathycaprino/2014/05/21/6-ways-pushing-past-your-comfort-zone-is-critical-to-success/#551dc3d57e48>

16 Broks, P. in Brown, J., 2018, 'Philosopher offers a radical different perspective about life in a viral TED talk', *Ideapod*, <www.ideapod.com/philosopher-offers-radical-different-perspective-viral-ted-talk/>

17 Baggini, J., 2011, 'Julian Baggini: Is there a real you', *TED*, <www.ted.com/talks/julian_baggini_is_there_a_real_you?language=en>

18 www.medicalxpress.com/news/2018-12-zone-lifetime-professionals.html

19 Mihaly Csikszentmihalyi, 2008, *Flow: the psychology of optimal experience*, Harper Perennial Modern Classics

20 Maslow, A. H., 1971, *The farther reaches of human nature*, New York: The Viking Press, p. 269

21 Oxford English Dictionary

Audiobook

Get Into Your True Comfort Zone
is also available in audio format.

Jump onto your favourite audiobook platform
to have the story narrated for you by the author.

www.ingramcontent.com/pod-product-compliance
Lightning Source LLC
Chambersburg PA
CBHW022011290426
44109CB00015B/1141